Sailing
An
Informal
Primer

Richard Ulian

VNR Van Nostrand Reinhold Company
New York Cincinnati Toronto London Melbourne

Drawings by Cathryn A. Wright

Copyright © 1982 by Richard Ulian

Library of Congress Catalog Card Number 81-10381

ISBN 0-442-28665-1

Printed in the United States of America

Designed by Ginger Legato

Published by Van Nostrand Reinhold Company
135 West 50th Street
New York, NY 10020

Van Nostrand Reinhold Limited
1410 Birchmount Road
Scarborough, Ontario M1P 2E7, Canada

Van Nostrand Reinhold Australia Pty. Ltd.
17 Queen Street
Mitcham, Victoria 3132, Australia

Van Nostrand Reinhold Company Limited
Molly Millars Lane
Wokingham, Berkshire, England

16 15 14 13 12 11 10 9 8 7 6 5 4 3 2 1

Library of Congress Cataloging in Publication Data

Ulian, Richard.
  Sailing: an informal primer.

  Includes index.
  1. Sailing.   I. Title.
GV811.U44   797.1'24   81-10381
ISBN 0-442-28665-1
ISBN 0-442-28789-5 (pbk.)   AACR2

To A. P. H.
sailor and friend

Contents

1. Waterborne *1*
2. Sailing is Simple *4*
3. Beat, Reach, and Run *9*
4. Preparing to Solo *11*
5. Sailing Alone *14*
6. The Smaller, the Better *17*
7. Getting from Here to There *21*
8. Anchoring and Docking *28*
9. Too Much Wind *35*
10. Danger in a Small Boat *40*
11. A Sail to the Vineyard *47*
12. The Only Way to Buy a Boat *53*
13. Varnish and Truth *59*
14. Race, Anyone? *65*
15. Racing Hints for a Beginner *71*
16. A No-Sail Day *76*
17. Sails *86*
18. Wind and Calm *97*
19. Tide *102*
20. The Other Side of the Cape *110*
21. One Small Boat: A Passage through Time *117*
22. The Cruise of the Argo *132*
23. Companionship and Sailing *141*
24. Finish Line *143*
    Index *146*

Cape Cod

Boston

Duxbury

Plymouth

Middleboro

Saga
Br
Sagamo
Cape Cod Canal
Sand
Onset
Bourne
Bourne Bric

Pocasset

Megansett

New Bedford

West Falmouth

Waquo

Falmouth

BUZZARDS BAY

Quisset
Great Ne
Woods Hole

East C
Oak E

MARTHA'S
VINEYARD Edgartow

MASSACHUSETTS BAY

Race Point
Provincetown
Marblehead
North Truro
Highland Light
Lond Point
Wood End

Wellfleet

OUTER BEACH

Nauset Light
Nauset Coast Guard Station

ATLANTIC OCEAN

CAPE COD BAY

Rock Harbor
Namskaket Creek
Nauset Inlet
Sesuit Creek
Orleans
East Brewster
Bass Hole
Dennis
Pleasant Bay
Barnstable
Bass River
CAPE COD
Harwich
Chatham Channel
Bass River
West Dennis
Harwich Port
Channel
Hyannis
West Yarmouth
Allen's Harbor
Stage Harbor
Osterville
Hyannis Port
Morris Island
uit
Wianno
Point Gammon
Poponesset
Collier's Ledge
Bishop & Clerks
Pollock Rip Channel
Bell 5
Monomoy Point
Pollock Rip
connesset Shoal

NANTUCKET SOUND

Nantucket

NANTUCKET

Wianno Senior

Waterborne

•

Why sail? Or row, paddle, or mess around in a boat at all?

Because it brings peace. Contentment. Satisfaction.

It will get you outdoors. Where it is quiet. The air is fresh. Even salty.

And you will exercise. Use dormant muscles. Bend. Stretch. Pull. Balance.

And all this will happen while you are afloat on the surface of a simply marvelous element: water.

A boatman can hardly praise water enough. It effortlessly supports huge yachts lying motionless in the slip at dockside. But let just one outboard pass, leaving only a six-inch wake, and each yacht gently dips and sways, so delicately does this magical surface balance these great masses.

Stand on the dock and put your hand on a sixty-foot-long, forty-ton yacht. Gently, steadily push it. This house-sized object almost imperceptibly slides away until the dock lines take up. Such are the wonderful properties of water that one person can cause this bulk to move upon it.

Stand watch on the yacht club dock when the hurricane's edge sends short steep waves across a mere half mile of open, shallow bay. The thirteen-foot Whaler outboards buck like wild horses, tugging their painters tied to the floats. The floats themselves do a serpentine dance atop the chop and finally break apart at the butts. They swing at odd angles, the motorboats herding together, huddled, rubbing sides in the mayhem of marching white-frothed furrows.

Another time you will find yourself in deeper water offshore, where the fetch is ten miles, fifteen, twenty. Let the fresh sou'wester blow and the waves rise up to meet and slap your boat heartily. Fingers of spray cross the deck, coating your face, trickling under your foul-weather gear. When the next big wave approaches, a whoop of delight and anticipation goes up from those riding the rail. But, mysteriously, this one slides by noiselessly, on its way to another, more leeward rendezvous.

The water's surface has numerous guises—who can relate them all? Off the southern tip of Ireland, near Fastnet Rock, compressed by sixty-mile-an-hour winds into a shoaling Irish Sea, it rises into hulking waves thirty or more feet high depending on where you sight from and on what angle your boat rides. Big and steep and threatening, the top six feet of these waves—the breaking curl—can roll a boat over if caught just right. When the boat rights itself, pulled by the weight of its heavily ballasted lower hull sections, the deck may be washed clean of men, mast, and equipment. One recent summer night between midnight and 8:00 A.M., seventy-seven sailboats racing to Fastnet were rolled beyond horizontal; several rolled 360 degrees. Fifteen men did not come back.

Yet water gives life also. In it, we are told, life first formed, grew, diversified. The mysteries lying beneath its calm or stormy surface only heighten the fascination of floating in one's own boat atop the yielding, implacable substance. You feel glad to be alive. You are captain of your vessel for as long as you can deal with the many moods of the sea.

Sailing is Simple

•

I first taught small-boat sailing when I was twelve years old, at a camp on the north shore of Cape Cod. One of the directors of that camp was not a sailor, though he was a good athlete in his younger days and an enthusiastic, successful camp leader. His name was, honorifically, Captain Delahanty. The camp had a nautical flavor, its chief pride being a fleet of eighteen sailboats.

Some of these boats were flat-bottomed skiffs about twelve feet long, skittish and frisky as puppies. In half a breeze, especially with a heavy person's weight slightly to leeward, they would go right over. We used to do it for fun.

One day a typically fresh Cape Cod southwest breeze

was rippling the bay. We had just finished a race at our new sister camp about half a mile up the beach. I was asked to sail Captain Del back to camp in one of the skiffs. Our course was almost dead downwind.

I was scared of Del to begin with. He was jolly but ran a no-nonsense camp. He did not like accidents, especially boating accidents; the potential for damage to the camp was so high. I wanted to tell Robby Robinson, who ran the camp waterfront, that in this breeze Del might be better placed in one of the sixteen-foot knockabouts. But Del quickly hopped into the boat and with a grin and a wave called "I'll see ya' there" to those still ashore. He was fully dressed, about fifty years old, around two hundred pounds, agile on land, but rarely seen in a boat.

Off we went at a speed I could barely control. Del sat forward on a small seat astride the centerboard box. In the cramped, unfamiliar quarters it was awkward for him to move. Our speed kept increasing as we got further off the beach. I could feel Del's grin freezing. The little skiff was yawing and oscillating. I was standing in the stern, tiller between my knees, shifting my own small weight side to side, wondering what to say and do when we tipped over.

At this moment I think I grasped something about the simplicity of teaching sailing: I said absolutely nothing. Del, an instinctive athlete and alert human, began to lean his weight with me this way and that, opposing the flighty tilts of the little skiff. We soon reached a point about a quarter mile offshore from our moorings.

Some of the larger, more stable knockabouts full of kids were happily jibing just inshore of us, rapidly changing direction by sending the stern across the wind, to the accompaniment of some cheerful screams.

I knew if we jibed, Del and I would surely go over.

5

He turned to me with a question.

"Why don't we aim for the moorings, like the rest of them?"

He raised his arm to point, and the motion alone almost put us over. The wind had been freshening all the time. I bit my lip.

"Ready to—er—jibe," said I, casting a glance at Captain Delahanty.

"Ready," said he. But he had picked up my apprehension and maintained a tight grip on the thwart.

I saw my duty. Slowly I eased the skiff through the stages of broad reach and reach before I put the helm down. Come about is what we did, carefully turning into the wind so the boom would cross above Captain Del's head gently as we changed direction. Then we proceeded carefully on the new tack towards our mooring.

Although Del thanked me warmly for the sail, I saw his puzzlement. He knew something was different about our method of changing tacks. But subsequently he seemed more relaxed about camp sailing activities. Not so often did the red No Sailing flag fly when the wind blew hard. We were a little freer to venture beyond the buoys that marked the normal sailing boundaries. It was more fun.

I learned that a new sailor needs confidence most of all. The best way to achieve this confidence is to do only what will almost certainly succeed, at least at first. An instruction program will take many leaps forward that way. Or at least, few backward.

I do not know if Captain Del would have subscribed to the above. I never saw him in a sailing boat again!

Summertimes on Cape Cod nowadays I run a little sailing school. I have taught sailing on and off for almost forty years, and the more I teach, the simpler I think sailing is to learn. It can, however, be made to appear fairly complicated. Have you ever seen a diagram of the parts of the boat? Studied the rules of the road? Attended a classroom lecture on safe boating? Then you know what I mean.

Initially, you need to know nautical names for only about ten parts of the boat. Several are familiar: *stern*, the back of the boat; *bow*, the front of the boat; *mast*, the rigid vertical support for the sail; and *rudder*, the blade in the water, controlled on board by the *tiller*, that steers the boat. Most people are also familiar with *port*, the left side of the boat, and *starboard*, the right side of the boat, but get confused over which is which. To keep track, remember that port and left both have four letters.

Rope is called *line*. The lines used to set a sail's angle to the wind—to *trim* a sail—are called *sheets*. Main sheet trims the mainsail; jib sheets trim the jib. What is the *jib*? That small sail forward of the mast.

One more and you are done. *Halyards* are lines used to haul sails up the mast.

That about covers the complete parts-of-the-boat course. It takes a minute or two to learn while we stand in the cockpit of the boat. The rest of the nomenclature comes naturally in the normal progression of sailing.

For instance, I ask a new student to take off the *stops* from the mainsail. He looks puzzled. What stops? Nobody mentioned stops. But a glance toward the ties wrapped around the furled sail explains what stops are. Soon the mainsail is hoisted and so is the jib. I ask one person to take the tiller. I go forward to cast off the mooring.

I generally walk the mooring back so we will sail off in a direction clear of other boats. After I drop it, I take my time returning to the cockpit. Meanwhile, the helmsman is sailing the boat quite independent of any obvious aid from

7

teacher. This makes for a contented, eager student. I wait as long as possible before offering suggestions. I find reason to compliment the new sailor's steering ability—steering is not difficult. Sometimes I don't touch the tiller until we return to the mooring, and if the wind is favorable and the student quick, not even then. He moors the boat.

Going back to the dock in the Whaler is one happy student sailor.

"It's really quite simple," an eight-year-old young lady said to me this summer as she merrily sailed us back to shore in her family's Laser after tip-it-over practice.

It really is.

Beat, Reach, and Run

•

If sailing is so simple, what can be learned on the first sail? Basically, to steer and to have fun. To run free, reach, and beat. To make a couple of passes at the mooring if conditions are right.

To *run*, or *run free*, is to sail in a downwind direction. The wind comes from behind the boat. The sail is let out wide enough to catch it with maximum efficiency. Almost every student sailor can do this correctly right away. Next time out, however, most do not let the sails out far enough. One does have to keep alert to the direction of the wind flow. When it is directly from behind, set the sails out wide.

When the wind blows at a right angle to the boat's course—over the beam—the sail goes about halfway out.

This is called *reaching*, a most comfortable point of sail. Almost all boats sail fastest reaching.

You want to make progress into the wind's direction—upwind. You can, though not directly into it. Trim the sails. Steer a course as close upwind as you can, keeping the sails full and the boat driving. This is close-hauled sailing, called *beating* when you go off a ways on one tack, then back on the other, so making zigzag progress upwind.

Why give names to these attitudes of the boat's course relative to the wind? Because the names are a useful short-hand for things you will have to do if you are going to get from place to place in a sailboat.

On some days when the wind is from the north, we cast off the mooring in the bay. The channel leads southward toward the cut into Nantucket Sound. We will have to run free down the channel. Fine, an easy ride. We let out the sail wide and go straight on out.

The shoreline runs roughly east-west. We decide to go west against an incoming tide. West we turn . . . and reach we must, since the north wind now comes over our beam. We trim the sail halfway and take off at maximum speed.

Coming home, we must reach back to the cut, the sail on the other side of the boat, tide behind us. Then close-hauled, making short zigzags port tack then starboard, each as close to the wind's direction as we can manage, we beat all the way up the channel to our mooring. Finally, we swing directly into the wind and coast to a stop at the mooring buoy.

Beat, reach, and run. If you have to get from here to there and back, you will normally do all three.

Preparing to Solo

·

Next time you sail, study the wind more closely. What direction is it coming from? Does it vary? Much? Constantly?

It does vary. More than a little. Hills around the bay will bend the wind. So will buildings, a grove of trees, other boats. Even if unobstructed over a large expanse of water, the wind will usually swing through five-, and sometimes to twenty-, degree oscillations. And the interval between shifts is normally short—not more than several minutes.

Some days major changes occur. The old wind dies and a new one ripples in. A 180-degree change can occur within moments, or the wind may "veer" (change in a clockwise direction) or "back" gradually.

Weather experts have provided excellent explanations for these shifts. The overall movement of high and low pressure systems plays a part in the larger changes. Patterns that develop within these systems contribute to local wind vagaries, as do topographically and thermally induced currents, updrafts, and downdrafts. We shall take a look at some of these patterns later.

But at the outset the important thing for a sailor to understand is that *wind rarely blows from a steady point of the compass*. The rule is to observe, be sensitive, remain alert to each change and shift. Better sailing will result.

Let's set off on our second sail. On the way out to the boat we mark the wind's direction. Moored boats generally swing to the wind, unless, of course, the wind is light and an opposing current stronger. Flags flying, smoke, telltales on mastheads will confirm your observation. In very light air, when all hangs motionless, wet your finger and hold it up. It will feel coolest on the side where a faint breeze strikes it, evaporating the moisture. Whatever your method, keep checking the wind direction every two or three minutes.

With your instructor you rig the sails, cast off clear of other boats, and sail down the channel. Beat, reach, and run for a while. You easily learn to tack—to change course in such a way that the bow crosses the point from which the wind is coming, filling the sails on the boat's other side—and to *jibe*—to change course by sending the stern across the wind's direction, again filling the sails on the boat's other side. You will see how to control the main sheet on a jibe, keeping loose-fingered so the line pays out smoothly. You will learn to stay alert during a jibe, when your head or upper body can be struck by the boom.

Find an isolated buoy or a lobster pot and practice mooring. Easy does it. Approach so that, when you swing directly upwind, the gliding boat stops just about at the buoy. A bit of practice is what it takes.

On our third lesson, you again first note the wind direction, then rig, cast off, beat, reach, run, tack, jibe, and moor. You learn to steer backwards, by reversing the tiller when the boat moves backwards. And you will master the rudiments of anchoring, an operation similar to mooring except that, when the boat's forward motion stops, you lower the anchor and make sure it sets well and will not drag readily.

Next time out you may learn how to pick up a man overboard, much like picking up a mooring. You will tie four or five knots, all the knots you will need to know for pleasure sailing: half-hitch, clove hitch, bowline, square, and reef. And you might want someone to show you how to whip rope ends to prevent unraveling. You sail, sail, sail. You now really feel comfortable and pleased with your progress.

Next lesson, if the wind is not heavy, you will solo. After half an hour of aimless but pleasurable sailing, you will be given a destination. Count on a beat and a run, maybe a reach. You do it easily, sail back, and land the boat on the launch or on a mooring buoy.

You can sail now. All you need is practice—alone.

Sailing Alone

•

I like to sail alone. Almost everyone does. Who would not feel the enjoyment and satisfaction it brings? Alone, in command, effortlessly floating across the water's frictionless buoyancy, propelled by the silent wind.

Because of its serenity, single-handed sailing often provides particularly pleasant memories. I recall one particular day, beating down-channel and out into Nantucket Sound in our Wianno Senior. The summer sou'wester had set in: fifteen or eighteen knots of smoky breeze, temperature in the eighties, whitecaps, and a two-foot chop, just enough to send spray over the bow. A perfect day. A day to sail.

About a half mile offshore I ease the sheets and reach off for Bell Five, a buoy marking the edge of Horseshoe Reef, well out past Collier's Ledge. No other boats are close. My own world, to do with as I please. I stand, sit, and wander about after tying the tiller so the boat will self-steer. I lie on my back in the cockpit, looking up at white sails and blue sky. Nothing was ever so white, nor so blue. After a while I climb down into the cuddy for some food or a soft drink or a tool with which to do some minor piece of maintenance. If the boat is steering herself well, I go up and lie belly-down on deck, watching the bow wave as it curls and froths. I take a full dousing and gasp when the chop hits just right, but the sudden dash of cold water is followed by the quick heat of the sun.

Before I close Bell Five I cross paths with the Oak Bluffs ferry or another sailboat coming down the sound toward Hyannis. I realize the time has come to head back, deflating for a moment. But then it is a glorious reach back to the stone jetties of the Osterville cut. I will be home in time for supper.

Coming up the channel it is a straight run, the boat carrying me in motionless flight like some great soaring bird. In the gold-touched ambience of late afternoon on West Bay I hear only the whoosh and bubble of water parting under the hull.

At the mooring I line up the Senior carefully before swinging into the wind. Heavy and strong, she will carry a long way in smooth water. While she glides, I should have plenty of time to walk to the bow, flatten down on my stomach, and pick up the mooring buoy.

When I finally have furled the sails, put the boat to bed, and returned in the Whaler to the dock, I dawdle, stopping to look back at the harbor one more time. I feel contented. The wind has died. In the soft light of evening sun white hulls glisten and glow; a leafed cove stripe catches a last slanting ray and sends back a star-shaped flash. All is peaceful and well with the world.

6

The Smaller, the Better

·

How big a boat can one person handle alone? How small a boat can you have fun in? I believe a twenty-five-foot boat is about the maximum size that one sailor can handle pleasurably through all likely conditions. The United States Coast Guard defines a small boat as one under twenty-five feet, and a big boat, presumably, is one over that length. Our Wianno Senior is exactly twenty-five feet long, making her, I suppose, neither small nor big. She keeps one busy enough.

On the other hand, much depends on rig, purpose, and experience. Alone, Joshua Slocum took *Spray* around the world. She measured thirty-six feet. Sir Francis Chichester's second boat was twenty feet longer. That seems huge until you remember *Vendredi*, the 113-foot three-master that Dick Carter designed a few years ago for the single-handed transatlantic race. She was sailed across successfully, though the rig proved too exhausting for one man to handle, and she did not win. I suppose one sailor could sail a boat even larger than *Vendredi* in open water. But anchoring, mooring, raising and lowering sails, docking—all the things we frequently do when sailing for pleasure—present fairly strenuous problems to the single-handed sailor in almost any boat over twenty-five feet, particularly in strong winds.

The beginner wants to find the smallest boat possible. Small boats are quick and sensitive to respond yet do the least damage when mishandled. They make ideal beginners' boats. If the boat is big enough to sit stably and semicomfortably in, then it is big enough. For adults, this often turns out to be a boat of about twelve feet. Beetle-cats, a popular class of about that length in my area, make great boats for adult beginners. An eight-foot pram works well for a small youngster who can tuck himself into it comfortably.

When learning to sail, nothing compares to sailing by yourself. Once you have had enough instruction to solo, you have had enough instruction for a while. You will not further learn to sail from a book nor from lectures and chalk talks. Certainly not from movies or slides. Nor by prolonging sailing with an instructor.

Alone, you have time to observe, experiment, err, correct. Each solitary moment teaches its lesson better than if accompanied by the instructor's now superfluous voice. Just find the boat, choose the winds and place that comfortably match your experience, and go.

The hardest part of the equation often is finding a boat. A sailing school will sometimes let you rent one as part of its course. Your instructor may know of boats available. Sailing clubs and community associations in the larger cities are excellent sources not only for boats but for basic instruction. Eventually you may have to—may want to—buy your own boat.

I would not recommend boardboats—the small sailboats that look like a surfboard rigged with a sail—for adults to learn or practice on initially. They lack inherent stability. The sailor provides the hull with stability in the form of his own weight . . . movable ballast. This can be tricky for a mature adult, though youngsters seem to handle it fairly well.

Beachside concessionaires have been known to send beginners out in boardboats or very small sailboats with a cheery "good luck" and not much else. Even if they do keep an eye on you, chances are good you will be an unraveled, shaken-up beginner upon returning to shore, all confidence lost after an hour or two of wrestling—more in the water than on it—with a supposedly simple boardboat in a breeze. Do not try to sail boardboats— or any boats for that matter—in much over seven knots of wind unless you have the competence to benefit from and enjoy the experience.

Inexpensive, well-designed, and sporty, boardboats and small sailboats have shown a phenomenal growth rate. In the past twenty years, 150,000 Sunfish have been built for United States sailors. In 1979, 12,000 Windsurfers, 10,000 Sunfish, and almost 4,000 Lasers were sold in the United States, ranking them first, second, and fourth respectively among the fastest growing classes of boats. In · third place was the Hobie 16, a catamaran. Catamarans ranked fifth, sixth, and seventh as well.

Surely Windsurfers and similar boardboats will continue to increase their sales totals greatly in the next few years. The Windglider was chosen for Olympic competition in 1984. Catamarans and trimarans are also winning not only popularity but respectability in the once proud and disdainful world of monohulls; witness the trimarans' complete domination of the 1980 OSTAR transatlantic single-handed race.

Many types of boats are available for learning and practicing. A boat that is well built and well designed will provide lots of fun and plenty of opportunity to learn. Find the smallest one on which you feel comfortable, can sit comfortably, and feel secure stepping aboard.

Then sail!

7

Getting from Here to There

·

Getting somewhere in a sailboat is not that hard. It may take more time than using engine power. It may not. It will normally take patience. Planning will help.

My point is much difficulty can be attached to an essentially uncomplicated and pleasant process. If you can sail your boat safely and successfully in local waters, you can sail it almost anywhere.

But do consider the *if*. I recall a man who did not. One summer morning I got a call from his wife. She and their twelve-year-old son had taken three lessons from me during the previous week. They were both bright, quick learners. She especially had impressed me because she could not swim yet concentrated fully on what we were learning, never wavering in the very strong breezes of that week.

Her husband had just bought a new boat from a dealer in Arey's Pond. I knew the place because my own boat was stored at the boatyard there when I bought her. I needed four days to sail her home, a distance of about thirty miles, including two days sitting in Chatham harbor waiting for the fog to lift and a long, single-handed sail around Monomoy Point over an Atlantic graveyard at Pollock Rip.

But her husband had never sailed nor been on a boat at all except as crew with friends. He was an exceptionally intelligent, confident, and aggressive businessman in his middle thirties. He bought the boat, a twenty-three-foot production cruiser with an auxiliary nine-horsepower outboard, and cheerfully announced to his wife and son that they would now sail it to Osterville. He would be the skipper.

His wife called me after three days. They had safely gained Allen's Harbor, leaving about fifteen miles to go. But the sails had not even been up yet. They had powered down Pleasant Bay, skinned through behind Morris Island on a full high tide, saving the trip through Pollock Rip, and powered along near the beach to Harwich Port. After an unsuccessful attempt the next day to power against a fresh sou'wester, they had put back into Allen's Harbor. Would I please come down, help sail the boat back, and give them a lesson? She sounded a little concerned.

I looked out the window, knowing full well the pines' branches were tumbling and shaking—another twenty-five-knot day, the fourth or fifth in a row. I had returned the night before from a Marblehead-to-Plymouth delivery and lesson with a husband, wife, and two young sons. I did not feel at all like doing it again, but still . . . the next morning I found myself in their station wagon pulling into the Allen's Harbor parking lot.

Now here, patently, was a guy who should not—could not—sail his boat under such conditions. Sending his wife and son to me for a few lessons had not helped much. You really do have to know how to sail before you can sail from here to there.

We had a long, tough day despite the fact I had sailed the route often. It blew hard. Off Point Gammon, it blew even harder and veered west, nearly on the nose for us. I took us all the way out to Bishop and Clerks to get a better slant and to wait for a favoring tide. In that particular boat, sailing that far out against the stiff breeze and steep waves was like beating to Bermuda. They were a gutsy family and marvelously good-natured, but most of my energy went towards keeping panic out of the boat. The puffs laid the high-sided, tender hull over time after time. Nothing much I did made the going easy. When we finally entered West Bay at around 5:00 P.M., I was as relieved as they were. The wife, writing a check for the ample amount I asked, added more. She felt they would not have gotten home without help.

I agreed. The man should never have tried it. His life, his wife, and his son were on the line. He would not have attempted to drive a car that distance without previous driving experience; why would he try to sail it? Surely not to avoid the overland trucking charge . . . which he ended up paying to me in any case.

But once you do know how to sail, little should deter you from taking a trip. The longest voyage is done one mile at a time. If you can sail one mile well, you can sail the rest of them.

Not much extra equipment is needed for coastal cruising beyond a full-sized government chart, available at most marine supply stores. Study it for a couple of hours the evening before leaving, getting the hang of the depths, buoy markings, and compass roses. Better not fool around with the miniaturized charts bound in book form. These can lead to reading mistakes under pressure. And each book includes lots of charts you will not need. You wind up paying more for less useful material.

Have aboard a compass that works. Even on a fairly clear day, from only a couple of miles offshore, your own harbor will often be hard to pick out by eye alone.

Depth sounders, radio direction finders, other electronic navigation aids, ship-to-shore radios—all are unnecessary on short coastal trips in small boats. They will malfunction or distract, either way needlessly complicating your trip.

Stow good lifejackets, one for each person. Boats with large leaks and small pumps can and do sink. Tow your dinghy if on a long trip. It serves both as a lifeboat if needed and as a ferry to shore at your destination.

Plan to sail about three or four hours a day. Reserve time for a swim, shore exploration, lunch in a cove, cocktails, dinner. Sailing is fun and relaxing. But, like anything else, it becomes monotonous in overly large doses, especially for your companions, who may not feel charged with such exciting and satisfying responsibilities as the skipper. Give them time to have other kinds of fun.

This involves bringing decent food and drink or planning to stop where they are available. If I am skipper or crew, I do not use beer, liquor, or drugs that alter mind or body until the day's sailing is done. It seems foolish to me to suppress judgment and agility while discharging a task for which they are needed. And why displace the natural high of sailing your boat with the buzz of a drug?

Check the weather. Not necessarily the forecast (although it is interesting to compare it with what later actually happens), but the weather itself. If you find it is too windy, calm, cloudy—too anything—postpone. You must feel comfortable with the conditions of the day, or sailing is not very simple, nor will the trip be very safe.

Setting a destination that merely requires an easy reach can help make for a pleasant journey. With some luck you may have a reach again on returning. But this is so generally unpredictable a proposition that sometimes you will do just as well to pick a place you especially want to see, whatever the wind direction. If the wind is not favorable, plan at least to sail with a favoring tide.

The tide is predictable, and sometime during any given day it may be going your way. If your course cuts directly across a tidal current, sail near the slack, when the tide turns and there is almost no current, at flood or ebb. Your course will be shortened by as many miles as the average current-per-hour multiplied by the hours it takes to cross the distance. Though speed is not your object, you will avoid the frustration of sailing for twice as long a time (and twice as far over the bottom) as another boat making the same trip on a more favorable tide.

If available, study a tidal current chart for your area. You will find surprising ways to use the tide. Where it splits against a shore, you can time your coastwise passage to ride the last three hours of the outgoing current to the midpoint, then catch the next three hours of the incoming current continuing in the same direction. Such a split, a famous one, occurs off Newport, Rhode Island. The ocean is full of such oddities, and coastal sailors can enlist, rather than fight against, their effects.

In a small boat cruising the coast, fog seems to me an exaggerated menace. It looks worse than it is. You have got a compass. You know where you want to go. Your chart tells where any buoys you might sight are located, and the course to the next one is clear on the chart. Unless running tide carries the boat more or less distance than allowed for, the course you set should work. If the current does set you too far and you miss the next buoy, you are not lost. You know generally the direction of the land. Head for it, getting in close enough to make out a shape on shore. Take an educated guess whether to turn right or left for your harbor. Check water depths visually or by poking an oar or heaving a weight on a marked line. Proceed slowly. If totally stumped, anchor. Under normal conditions, fog is not accompanied by a storm. When greeted with patience and calm, it brings no great harm.

When thick fog and stormy winds combine and you are closing a lee shore, you do have to pay extremely careful attention. Before the storm and scud roll in, mark where you are on the chart, the correct time, the compass course to refuge, and your speed over the bottom. If you have to come head-to-wind to douse sail—and it may take some time—plot your off-course progress and fix a new compass heading. Average out the yaws and swings of the boat to reflect the course you are making good. Judge or measure your speed continuously and average it out. If you were four miles offshore and are making four miles an hour, it is wise to start listening hard for breakers on shore before an hour has elapsed!

Provided your harbor is clearly marked and not ringed with shoals, bars, or rocks, you have a good chance of getting in without mishap. But if you are headed for hazards, you may be better advised to stay off and sail around until the fog lifts, even though doing so invites some discomfort.

I have been caught in fog occasionally in a small boat. So have almost all the sailors I know. No one has been hurt by it. Embarrassed, yes. Puzzled. Even temporarily lost. Maybe aground. But not hurt.

You will eventually emerge from even the thickest fog bank, the harbor you have been seeking (or maybe another one) not too far distant.

And very likely—even though it was not all that difficult—you will feel proud of sailing safely from there to here.

·8·

Anchoring and Docking

·

Watching another boat anchor or dock is always fun. The potential for foul-up is high; for danger, low. It is a second-guesser's paradise. Count on having in your audience everyone who is topside in the harbor fleet and half the people within line of sight ashore.

Sailboats do not have brakes. This is the source of much onlooker enjoyment and, I think, has more to do with a beginning sailor's uneasiness than any other factor, more even than the angle of heel (or tilt) the hull naturally assumes. A beginner quickly perceives that the boat easily moves forward. But subconsciously he feels the lack of a reliable means to stop. He remains silently apprehensive. Eventually the instructor tells him to let the tiller go. The boat docilely swings into the wind and glides to a stop. Relieved smile.

Coming up head-to-wind to stop at a selected spot is an art, which makes docking and anchoring touchy. The boat carries too far. Or not far enough. Then what? Go around and try again. Of course, if you had an engine, things would be easier. But engines quit and props foul. You really ought to be able to do it under sail.

Picking the right anchorage helps. Study the harbor chart. If still in doubt, rouse up the harbormaster or some local people to talk to. You want enough water to float clear at low tide but not too much depth for the anchor to hold well without excessive scope. And you need swinging room.

When you see your spot, slow down. You can then judge the boat's carry more easily. If the breeze is strong, drop a sail. Taking the jib down subdues a flapping monster-to-be on the foredeck. The person handling the anchor gear will also be able to work better.

Occasionally you will see someone with the guts to roar in under full sail, come up into the wind, and smartly drop the anchor in a crowded harbor. Though dashing and pretty from the spectator's viewpoint, I wouldn't encourage you to try it in a really large boat and a small harbor: anchoring then becomes difficult because a large boat may not have space to glide to a stop in a small harbor and because other boats are so close that maneuvering with all sails up becomes nearly impossible.

So, slowed down, possibly with one sail dropped, you round up into the wind. Wait until the boat stops fully. If you slowly lower the anchor to the bottom, it most likely will arrive unsnarled. The boat now falls backward, pushed by the wind. The anchor line is paid out and then

finally snubbed tight, so the flukes, the gripping blades on
the anchor, bite against the drag. You observe for a moment to see that you are not pulling the anchor along the
bottom. Let out line so the pull on the anchor is not angled
too sharply upward. A scope of seven times the water
depth is nice if the boat has room to swing. Down comes
the mainsail. Furl 'em up. Sit down in the cockpit and have
a beer.

The anchor gremlins will find you early in your career.
After a heavy nighttime squall you look out your harbor-
side hotel window and see that the boat has dragged clear
across to the other side of the harbor. Fortunately, as it
drags into shoaler water the scope ratio increases. The
anchor is pulled more on the level and its flukes bite better.
The boat probably will not go onto the beach, unless the
dropoff is extremely sharp. But it might get close enough
to scare you and possibly to mar the keel on a pebbly
bottom.

If strong current has more influence than light wind,
swing your boat up head-to-current, not head-to-wind.
Before dropping anchor, unsheet your sails. Get them
down quickly after dropping it, or you will sail merrily
around the anchor, creating a highly satisfactory mess—
from the spectator's vantage.

In some harbors tidal currents run in different directions or at differing strengths under adjacent boats. Edgartown is known for it. As the tide turns, the boats start a slow
dance. They lie alongside one another, head to toe, kissing,
rubbing, wrapping anchor lines. Not much damage results, and there are few recriminations, since the effect is
largely unpredictable.

Using a two-anchor Bahamian moor (one ahead, one
behind, then both lines led through the bow chocks, boat
swinging on the bridle) may be a cure worse than the

30

disease. No one uses this system in Edgartown, where the bottom is slippery mud. With the crowding and the dragging at regatta time, if many boats put down two hooks, I suppose it might be November before everyone got unwrapped.

In fact, even in the Caribbean I do not ever remember seeing a Bahamian moor. Lots of sailors write of using it; perhaps I just was not in the right place at the right time. Once, in the Tobago Cays, we anchored in the gap between Petit Rameau and Petit Bateau, a small space. Our chartered seventy-two footer and a fifty-foot cutter were the only two boats there. We both put out stern anchors. The current directly reversed. We had nosed in so far that when it turned eastward, our deep-draft boats might have swung on shoal ground at the east end. But the simple stern anchors held both boats steadily through the night. They were easy to get out the next morning too.

Getting the hook out is usually easier than anchoring. But if you are planning to return at the end of the day, and you have a spare anchor to sail with, you can just tie a plastic bleach bottle to the anchor line as a buoy and leave it.

Go slowly when taking the anchor up. Think about it first. Perhaps the only problem not obvious is that the mud has to be washed and scraped off while the anchor, and probably the person washing it, hang over the bow. Harbor mud often has a strong clammy smell, besides being loose and runny. You do not want it on your boat.

If your anchor line and someone else's are wrapped, apologize and unwrap them patiently. What gets tangled can normally be untangled. Next time you will anchor further away.

Did you ever watch an ocean liner or a freighter dock? The slowness of her approach is agonizing. How little speed the tugs allow her. These huge boats have poor brakes, and water offers little friction for stopping. The ship has to be stopped almost completely long before arriving at dockside.

The largest, heaviest vessel stops with greatest difficulty. But the same principle applies to the smaller boat. Its skipper must devise a method of arriving at the dock already stopped. If he does not, his landing will be accompanied by derogatory comments or—worse—dead silence from the inevitable audience, not to mention possible damage. It is an experience worth avoiding.

Proceed slowly, as in all anchoring and docking. Ease sheets before nearing the dock. You do not need the extra speed. This simplifies your calculations and lessens the problems if you still overshoot. Try to land on a float's outer end rather than in the middle between other boats: if your speed is too great, you can slide off on the free side and go around again.

Have a person on the bow ready to fend off, cushioning the potential impact by pushing the boat from the dock. Someone on the dock will usually do likewise. But if the approach speed gets really out of hand, have these people keep away from the space between dock and boat. Better to damage equipment than bodies.

One summer afternoon when I was thirteen my entire family went sailing out of Gloucester on a rented thirty-three-foot gaff sloop. I was skipper and sole sailor aboard. A boy from the boat docks who had accompanied us the preceding day had attested to my sailing ability so earnestly that the establishment's owner had given his permission for this arrangement. In view of my age, size, and unlined face, he was reluctant. Rightly.

We had a nice sail to the outer harbor and back. My father, mother, sister, and grandmother were quite at ease.

They did not seem to notice my mounting concern as we threaded through the inner harbor into the narrow end where the rental dock lay. The afternoon breeze was freshening, and the huge gaff main was driving that lovely white hull at a pretty bubbly clip.

I was one nervous kid. Other boats lined the float, hanging off it at right angles in the breeze. There was only about seventy feet of open water to swing up and stop in. I sailed across in front of the dock several times, looking it over. We were going like a Cup defender. A boy on the dock—my friend of yesterday—wore an expression combining grimace and prayerful hope. The owner stood behind, watching. My grandmother looked unperturbed, sitting on deck just forward of the mast, knitting.

One space remained at the float, between two sailboats. I sailed into an open patch to leeward as near the docks on the far side as I could. We were going much too fast. I did not think of easing the sheet—or perhaps I thought we were too close to the facing docks and might rip the big main or scrape the long, overhanging boom. Perhaps. But when I put the helm down we had a 150 feet of momentum and only about 30 feet of open water ahead. In a blink the bow had nosed between the boats on either side, committing us to going straight ahead.

My young mentor stood steadfast on the float, frantically instructing me to try to brake the boat with the rudder. No use. I was too young, too inexperienced, too unfamiliar with boats of this size—and going too fast!

We ran right up over the float as far as the mast step. The low float easily submerged as it lifted our bow. Despite her new elevation, my grandmother never stopped knitting. Everyone who had been standing on the float ran for safety except the boy, who made a quick futile effort to stop our momentum before jumping aside.

The owner glumly allowed that his boat would open up some and leak for the rest of the summer. And he had just had her caulked.

I did not sail a boat that large again for many years. When I did, I made sure to approach a dock slowly. In tight approaches, I reduced sail, or eased sheets, and I learned how to slow a boat with the action of the rudder.

Docking really is not so hard. Just do it in a boat you know and understand, in conditions you can handle. The same holds true for anchoring. Go slowly. Let the dock or the anchoring spot come to you, inch by inch. It will, and you will walk away with pride, dock, and boat intact.

9

Too Much Wind

·

One day toward the end of summer, after two weeks of cool, damp, northeast weather, the wind goes back into the southwest. And blows hard. The sun comes out and a light-diffusing haze surrounds everything. Smoke, we call it: a smoky sou'wester, the product of steamy, Gulf air blowing across the cooler waters of Nantucket Sound.

I take the moldy, mildewed clothing and shoes from the closet and place them on the porch to dry in the sun. This summer we live in a marvelously constructed, enclosed and converted water tower, the very paragon and pagoda of water towers, in fact, sweeping in graceful curved sections four levels high to a porched, railed and roofed summit eighty feet in the sky. It was redesigned some years ago by the young man of the property as his personal office, cottage, and general summer quarters. It stands free, about a hundred yards from the main house and perhaps twenty-five yards from two other cottages on the grounds, the whole situated not over a hundred yards from the water's edge at Wianno. A desultory-looking three-car garage, full of the detritus of this enterprising young man's youth, lies close by. But the gray, shingled structure, borne aloft by the magnificent curved six-by-fours of late-nineteenth-century Cape Cod carpentry, thrusts gracefully above it, above even the tallest of the neighboring pine trees.

No sailing lessons are scheduled today; my other work is caught up. We have lived here for only a few weeks, and I resolve to climb for the first time through the skylight to the tower's top to get a good look at the new weather that is upon us.

Even at the third level, I feel the tickling sensation that extreme height evokes in the back of my upper legs. I still have to climb a vertical ladder to the roof hatch, untie and raise it, and then climb through if I am brave enough. I ascend until my head and shoulders poke through the hatch opening and, slitting my eyes against the windblown pigeon guano and dust particles from the long undisturbed widow-walked roof, peer at a most impressive view.

I look down over two quite different seas. The first, of swaying pines, is solid green for a mile in every direction but south. Not a house shows through the clustered pines, so thick and tall do they grow. A half mile away, I can see the only other Wianno tower like mine. Its top shows above the sea of green, which waves in pale and dark shades as fields of long grass will do on a windy day.

The second sea, to the south, is Nantucket Sound, deep blue at its nearer reaches, then white-blue far off where horizon meets water, the whole surface absolutely frothed with whitecaps. Only two sailboats are out this morning, no doubt because of the wind's strength. They have just left the safety of Osterville cut and from this distance—perhaps a mile—look like toys politely nodding and bowing to each other in a store window.

Lots of wind today. The wind is surely twenty-five knots, gusting higher. I watch the two boats for a while. One, then the other, turns and runs back for the cut. They are small boats. Better to sail in the inner bays—shallow West Bay, the narrow Seapuit River protected by its dune barrier, Cotuit Bay, through the Narrows into wide, safe North Bay, and back under the drawbridge to a West Bay mooring. A pleasant sail, and today, all a small-boat sailor can handle without strenuous athletics and some discomfort.

I suppose that is the secret of heavy-weather sailing in a small boat: not to undertake more than you, or it, can handle. Unlike the ocean racer or offshore cruiser, who may be days or weeks from landfall and must take whatever weather comes, the small-boat sailor can choose. It is not a luxury to brush aside.

The amount of wind you can handle in a certain boat depends on many things: your skills, the boat's inherent stability and condition, wave heights, the nature of the shoreline and bottom, the size of the body of water, the direction of the wind. Your own common sense and emotions will be the best guides. Common sense should keep you out of extreme conditions: gale winds, lightning storms. On borderline days, if you are standing on shore feeling frightened and you are not accompanied by someone more experienced and secure, do not go. You have a good chance of losing more than you will gain from the experience. But if you feel fairly confident, although challenged, and can successfully visualize the sequences necessary to rig, cast off, sail, and most importantly, moor the boat, go. You will learn from it, even if there are some goof-ups.

The practical limit is the durability of the boat's gear. When the wind reaches gear-buster velocity—different for differing boats and even for the same boat handled by different sailors—stay put. Many small boats will start to break masts, booms, tillers, and blow out sails in winds of twenty-five or thirty knots.

Ten-knot winds travel about 11½ miles per hour. The number expressed is about 15 percent higher in miles per hour, as a nautical mile (knot) is about 15 percent longer than a land mile. Reversing this from miles to knots, a 23-mile-per-hour wind is blowing 20 knots, about 13 percent lower numerically, as the reduction in length of a land mile from a knot is about 13 percent. Increasing the numerical value (from knots to miles) use the 15-percent factor; decreasing, use 13 percent. If you can't remember which, use a compromise 14 percent factor to convert in either direction and you will not go wrong. Miles-per-hour will always be the higher number when expressing the same velocity.

At forty knots (forty-six miles per hour) experts can sail well-set-up small boats without breaking equipment or bodies. Several times I have seen six or eight of this country's better Laser sailors race most of the day in thirty-five knots of wind in protected waters. On those same days, while on patrol in a Whaler, I have helped to tow in twenty or more broken-down Lasers and their waterlogged skippers—all good, experienced sailors, but not quite that good. Few are.

Lots of sailors are seriously frightened by trying to negotiate heavy weather prematurely. I do not advise taking beginners out in more than fifteen-knot winds in small boats. Many a day on our bay the southwester fills in too strongly while the kids, beginners or intermediate-level sailors, three or four to a boat, are out taking lessons. Sometimes the instructions to start for home come a little bit late. The boats come careening back to the dock, running free, some of the kids white-faced and white-knuckled. A few of the landings can only be described as "crash." No great physical harm is done, but the mental damage hurts. The fear of being out of control, unable to steer, heeling too far, about to jibe, and heading straight for trouble is a fear that stays with a youngster too long. It is worth avoiding.

By the way, this is one time beginning sailors always seem to put their sails way out when running free. They feel that, since letting the sail out on a beat or reach slows the boat, it will do likewise on a run. It will not. What will slow the boat is to haul the sail *in* as far as possible, presenting less of its face to the wind. Sometimes this is hard to do, as a boat with a small rudder will want to round up when you trim in. Then you might just as well round up, drop the sails, and come in under a bare pole. The breeze pressing on the hull and rigging will move you downwind at a smart pace—sufficient for steering.

In general, avoid any conditions that frighten you. Be honest with yourself. When you can function in logical sequences of action, you and a good boat can handle almost anything you will encounter. But you must build up to it in gradual steps.

Any seasoned sailor can tell you his share of hairy weather stories. In fact he will be glad to. But do not plan to be involved in your own until you are ready and confident.

10

Danger in a Small Boat

·

In forty-seven years of sailing I have yet to see an injury that needed more than a bandage to fix. I have seldom even heard of more serious accidents in an area where I have sailed. There are plenty of spills, chills, dunkings, difficulties; excitement is not lacking. But the injury level is very low.

I am talking about recreational small-boat sailing in protected coastal waters and lakes. Offshore sailing or racing in any boat can create quite different circumstances.

A chief unlooked for danger among those that do exist for small-boat sailors seems to lurk on land—or over land—in the form of overhead power lines strung across parking areas. The last direction a sailor might look for danger in a parking lot is up. But power lines have been responsible for the deaths of several young people in recent years. The metal masts now in general use all too frequently extend to the height of many wires, especially if the boat is already sitting up on a trailer or being lifted. If the mast touches a live wire, instant death can result: anyone touching the boat can become a conduit to the ground for whatever electric current is carried by the wire.

Some boat manufacturers now place warnings at the mast step or partners. Perhaps soon all will. Sailing instructors should drive home the point. Parking ramps and rigging and launching areas obviously ought to be cleared of these hazards. If you see one that is not, talk to the management. Meantime, exercise caution!

Poor judgment can put you in danger any time, of course. Particularly, use care in matching the sailing conditions of the day with your experience level, as I have said before. Once that is done, little else threatens.

Lightning ought to be mentioned, though the chances of a strike on a boat are just as slim as on land. I have never seen a boat struck nor met anyone who claimed to, although I have read of such instances. Good sense would encourage one not to be near a tall object, the mast, surrounded by a level plain of water during an electrical storm. Get ashore if possible.

Most small sailboats now carry built-in flotation materials. The boats will fill with water but will not sink. Unballasted wooden boats without keels will usually float even when full of water. In the event of accident, so long as a boat floats, even nearly submerged, the best protection is to stay with it until rescued. In a heavily ballasted wooden boat or in a plastic or metal boat without flotation, life jackets are essential. For that matter, *every* boat should carry them. And people should not participate in water sports without being able to swim adequately, except perhaps under very controlled and guarded conditions.

Racing drastically increases the danger of collision. When the boats are much over sixteen feet long or are going fast, serious personal injuries can occur. On a race course with large yachts tacking close-hauled through a fleet of small boats, the chance exists of a small boat being blind-sided by a much larger yacht. The smaller boat will almost certainly be seriously damaged, its people thrown into the water. If you ever find yourself on a course like this, station one crew to leeward on lookout. Remonstrate with the race committee later.

In racing, a hidden danger, though rare, is a jibe by a boat close beside you. His boom sweeps very low across your cockpit. His crew is ready for a jibe. You and your crew may not be; in fact, you may have your backs turned to the danger. I have known people to be knocked out of their boats unconscious this way, with long-term injury resulting.

People do go overboard from small boats frequently, especially in races. Recovery is usually quick; it is no great trick to put a maneuverable small boat in position and make the pickup over its low freeboard. Sea and wind conditions are not usually extreme; long before a storm strikes full force, the small-boat sailor generally has picked up his mooring, snugged the boat down, and is watching the furies through a picture window.

Offshore yachts have a different problem. Far from safe harbor, they must slog through whatever the weather. A person overboard in ultimate conditions is a severe test and a touchy business to handle, much written of in books about offshore sailing. It seems clear that better safety harnesses and strong, integral tracks to clip them onto, running the deck's length, are going to be required. It is just too unrealistic to count on bringing exhausted crew back over the high-sided offshore boats, even if you can return and find them in time. It is a very chancy task.

The small-boat sailor, sailing for recreation in relatively safe waters, might do well to remember some special circumstances that do involve jeopardy for him. Single-handing is one. If a solo sailor falls overboard, especially when the boat is set up to self-steer, he has suddenly bought lots of trouble. Wearing a life jacket will help, but that still may leave a long swim home. Trail a line over the stern in rough conditions and you will have something to grab onto.

Be extra careful when you are the only adult sailing with young children. The risk is not so much that they will fall overboard—you and they will both be guarding closely against that—but that you might. It would put the youngsters in a very tough situation.

One flat, calm Monday when my sons, Mark and Steve, were eight and five years old, they accompanied me after a weekend of racing. We set out to deliver the boat from Harwich Port to Hyannis Port, perhaps ten miles, preparatory to the following weekend's regatta. The sea was so calm off Harwich Port that we accepted an offered tow from friends who already had their own Senior in tow. Within an hour the southwest breeze came on strongly, opposing the ebb tide. Near Point Gammon, off Hyannis, a steep four-foot sea developed. The Senior under tow ahead of us took some big waves over her bow that finally knocked the spinnaker pole loose. We were being thrown around in our boat too. I got the life jackets out of the cuddy and put them in the cockpit but not on the kids or myself.

The anchor was lashed on deck at the bow cleat. After

raising it, I had left it there for use at Hyannis Port. I went forward to secure it better, rigging a part of the half-inch anchor line tautly from the bow cleat back around the mast. This used some of the extra line that had been lying around on deck and helped make a firmer tie-down for the anchor.

Before long it became too rough to continue towing both boats. I put up the mainsail only. We were not quite around Gammon yet, but we cast off the tow and sailed for Hyannis Port.

The highest waves were now five or six feet, very sharp and steep. Several washed over our bow, loosening the anchor just enough to concern me. In hindsight, I should have left it. But I gave the tiller to Steve, already a fair sailor. I asked Mark to keep an eye on me and went forward.

I was facing aft working on the anchor lashings when I heard Mark yell.

"Look out, Dad! It's a monster."

Before I could look the deck dropped away from my feet in a dizzying motion. I gripped the line that I had lashed between cleat and mast and held it tightly. I was thrown clear overboard to leeward. The line I held stretched with the strain. Under the boat I went, looking up through solid green water. The wave passed, and I came to the surface, holding the line. Mark was kneeling almost above me holding out a life jacket.

"Luff up. Luff up!" I shouted.

Steve came up into the wind, and the next wave floated me back aboard, helped by Mark's strong tugs.

We were all sobered by that incident. We discussed what the boys would have done if I had been forced to accept the life jacket and swim for it. Could they have picked me up? Doubtful in those conditions, at their ages.

Could I have made it to the Gammon shore? Probably, with the jacket—it was less than half a mile, and the breeze was blowing onshore, although the tide was moving laterally and slightly offshore quite swiftly. Could they have sailed in alone? Most likely, but they might have had to beach the boat if they could not round Point Gammon.

Do not go forward, or to the extreme aft end of the boat either, in such conditions of weather and crew. If you must, be sure a strong lifeline is rigged and attach yourself firmly to it.

One other danger may not be obvious to beginning sailors. It occurs when a small, easily capsized boat, perhaps a boardboat, is sailed in a strong offshore breeze. This applies as well to a light rowboat or canoe, especially on a large body of water.

When the wind blows off the land, even at twenty-five knots or more, the water nearest the beach is only slightly rippled and flat and harmless-looking. The force of the breeze for several hundred yards outward is reduced by the shelter of houses, trees, and high ground. A beginner may quickly be misled. He sails handily out to where the full weight of the breeze is suddenly felt. Then he finds it is too much. Worse, the route back to safety now lies directly upwind. It also opposes the direction of the waves, which have grown large with the increase in distance offshore.

This can be a panicky situation. Should a boardboat capsize, it will be blown further offshore, very possibly at a faster rate of speed than an exhausted swimmer can maintain in attempting to catch it. A rescue is required, and if no rescue boat responds quickly, the potential for tragedy exists. When the wind blows offshore with strength, take extra care not to venture beyond your capabilities. If you are not yet expert, do not sail a boardboat in strong offshore breezes.

Small-boat sailing does have its dangers. Although they are few and infrequently result in accident, the penalties can be so great that careful thought and good judgment are required before setting out to sail.

11

A Sail to the Vineyard

•

The August day dawns sunny and warm. A southwest breeze has filled in, swaying pine branches in an increasing cadence.

From the windows of my converted water tower I watch the motion of the pine trees. By gauging the extent of the branches' sway, one can judge pretty well the weight of the wind and the state of Nantucket Sound.

Today I especially want to know these things. I plan to sail to Martha's Vineyard, about fifteen miles across the sound to Edgartown or perhaps ten to Oak Bluffs. I will sail wherever wind and tide allow.

At the club dock on West Bay the harbor chop is just beginning to show white caps. The windspeed indicator paddle on the clubhouse roof blurs as it spins—I would

47

guess about eighteen knots without going inside to read the dial. The Whaler's old Johnson 40 engine starts on the second try; good thing I changed the plugs again yesterday. After a short ride out to the mooring, sliding slowly past the rows of Beetles, the larger plastic auxiliaries, other Seniors, and several graceful older cruising boats in the outer tier, I reach a cluster of four Wianno Seniors lying snugly near the far shore. Ours, white topsides, bright-finished mahogany and oak trim, tan deck, is the last one in the line. As always when I pull the Whaler in behind the transom, I check her decks and hull for signs of something amiss: a loose line, a dent or nick, bad trim telling of excess water in the bilge. All looks well. I grab a handhold on her long, overhanging boom and step on. With a Senior's low freeboard, it is barely more than a level step from the Whaler bow to the sailboat deck. She is heavily built, stable, and moves minimally and pleasantly in the water under my weight.

In a moment's time I tie off the Whaler and throw foul-weather gear and sandwiches below. It's blowing harder already. Creaking noises tell a story of the wind's strength. Even here in the inner harbor, the boats are pitching busily in the chop. West Bay is shoal—nothing more than a ¾-mile square flat covered by thin water, with a six-foot-deep channel and various small mooring areas dredged out. The chop is sometimes quite short and steep.

Sail stops are quickly undone with a pull on the loose ends of the half-reef knots. The big gaff main unrolls to the cockpit floor. I stand on a seat and look around while putting in the battens: not much activity this weekday morning. Classes are beginning at the club dock, and the Beetlecats are loaded with kids. Crosby's tug is towing a beautiful blue Bermuda 40 towards her berth in Eel River. A couple of fishermen in work skiffs are clamming on the shoal at the channel bend off Wright's Point. It is half-tide. A typical summer morning on West Bay.

I put the picnic jib on and leave it lying loose on deck with the mooring buoy line thrown over so it will not blow off. Then, bracing my feet against the bulkhead, I grab the two halyards and haul up the main, keeping the gaff almost level until the sail is fully hoisted on the luff, then hoisting the gaff almost to its normal angle. The gaff peak will be hauled up further later as the halyards and sail stretch, but this will do for now.

I coil up the long halyard ends and stow them below, flat on the cuddy bench or hanging on a peg inside the bulkhead. The jib hoists easily, but then flogs, the clew shackle beating against the Sitka spruce mast, where I have placed protective strips of adhesive deck-surfacing material. I heard about a boat whose mast was so weakened by this beating that one day it fell like timber to the axe.

I walk the Whaler up and tie the painter to the mooring loop. Fortunately, the boat is just swinging away from those moored close by to starboard, so I cast off hurriedly and hop back to the cockpit with all possible speed. I arrive just after the main sheet begins to run out, and I jerk it into the cam cleat on its block, which secures it handily. I give the tiller a pull to keep her from heading up, and ease down to leeward to set the jib sheet in its cam cleat. Both ends of the jib sheets are tied together since I am alone today, and I bring the continuous looped line back with me as I finally sit down at the tiller. Under way.

The first puff stands the boat on her ear. Nearly dead still in the water, a heavy mass, she converts the wind's force first to heeling moment, then slowly to forward motion. I climb happily out on the gunwale, hanging beyond it, sitting on the hull side. I peer down at the boat's coppery red bottom, her long, shallow keel. We draw 2½ feet, centerboard up; it stays up until we reach deeper water outside the cut, a matter of policy in the shoal depths of the bay.

Slowly the boat settles back down, taking the wind, redirecting it with her sails, harnessing energy in the process, moving forward, heeling less. I climb in off the rail. The next good puff will send me out there again, exultantly riding this wildly tilting platform.

I concentrate on staying clear of moored boats. One tack carries the first leg of the channel past Garrison's Point. The next series of tacks takes me down the main segment to the cut. The tacks are short, the dredged channel being only about forty yards wide, but tacking is easy. The looped jib sheet can be jumped out of its cleat, and the new one cleated with little fuss. The main sheet stays cleated. On a boat of this size, this weight, a cleated main will cause no problem provided it can be released quickly if necessary.

On the beat puffs coming from the west over the high Oyster Harbors land heel the boat again. Solid water pours in over the coaming and runs out through the self-bailing scuppers in the cockpit. These are moments to remember: astride the high side, a foot hanging over the hull, the huge gaff main pressed well below eye level, a white wing curved against the blue water, carving the invisible wind. A shout pierces the rush of wind across the bay. Club kids in the Beetlecats turn and laugh. Was that you?

Outside the cut, the wind has lightened a little and backed to the south. The Vineyard can be reached in one long tack. I settle in on a course for Oak Bluffs. The tide is still going, as it is said on Cape Cod, meaning going out. This gives me an extra two knots of progress over the bottom. In a two-hour sail, two added knots mean more than four miles extra distance. Since Oak Bluffs is only eight or ten miles away, this is a big boost. Better still, the tide will turn just before I start back; I will have it both ways!

The sun is hot, the breeze smells fresh, clean, salty. Off comes my shirt and soon, when I get clear of shore and neighboring boats, whatever other clothing feels superfluous. I tie down the tiller with a loose end of the backstay pull. The boat balances well enough to steer herself for a while. I lie down on the cockpit sole, grainy but smooth, warm teak against my back. With a hand free to adjust the self-steerer, I take my course from the masthead telltale and the feel of the boat. The white curves of sail all but blot out the sky, the water burbles quietly around the hull.

Near Succonnesset Shoal I sit up to look around. I will be there in another hour—it does not really matter where. The wind picks up and backs further to the south. I can now lay off for Oak Bluffs. The sailing is without problems, but I must stay at the tiller, for my crude self-steerer works poorly on a reach. Two boats far to windward beat toward Edgartown. To leeward and ahead others round East Chop and harden up. They have a long beat to Edgartown against the last of the outgoing tide, whereas I reach comfortably past the breakwater, following the Hyannis ferry into the harbor at Oak Bluffs.

In the sheltered calm of the small circular harbor, I sightsee slowly among the moored boats. Three fishermen on the town landing watch. They appear curious about this gaff-rigged apparition ghosting through their harbor. When did a Senior last sail in here? A long time ago, to judge by their expressions.

I jibe in slow motion and buzz the dock, just coasting in the light air. Then, when we all have had a good look at each other, I head back out the narrow cut and set off on the return trip. It is a pretty harbor. Next time I will tie up at the dock and walk around.

On the way back the wind is further aft. I can broad-reach. A fast point of sail and a following tide make progress rapid. I am past Succonnesset and Great Neck in less than an hour; in double that time I am running free up West Bay, almost too quickly home. I hate to see it end.

It has been a grand sail. Long after the last summer race is forgotten, I will remember it: the way the puffs off the Oyster Harbors shore heeled the boat, the sails against water and sky, the pleasure of going somewhere—anywhere—traveling effortlessly across the surface of the water, itself moving silently, majestically in great tidal surges.

12

The Only Way to Buy a Boat
·

You do not pick a boat to buy. A boat picks you.

You declare yourself eligible, scout the boatyards, attend the boat shows, talk to anyone who will listen, and finally you meet a boat you cannot get out of your mind.

It will not do to skip the looking around. Not just at new boat shows and in old boatyards, but from waterfront restaurant windows; along the docks, in harbors; in sailing magazines and classified ads; and under winter covers. Somewhere inside you is a feeling for what a boat should look like. Finally you will find it.

Even if you have the spare cash to write a check for a shiny showroom beauty, I do not think you should do it. The boat would not be right for you. When you get to know it, hidden bad habits will surface. You will not spend much time together. You will eventually divorce.

Why so personal? For one thing, you trust your life to it. Reason enough. For another, boats are pretty. They have more compound curves than almost any other man-made object. When these are finely designed and built, a thing of beauty, even art, emerges; a Fyfe, a Herreshoff, a Crosby, a Frers, others.

Your boat may be of sound planking or fiberglass and plastic or have an aluminum hull, in perfect shape. It may, on the other hand, need new paint, ribs, deck, rig, gelcoat—two years of backyard work before the first sail. Fine, if that is your pleasure.

Try to be sure you are in love, not merely infatuated. You are going to spend lots of time with her and a greater amount of money than you planned. You are trusting her to give you a lot in return.

Let me tell you how my boat picked me. We had taken a cottage on Cape Cod at Harwich Port during the month of July. We had three kids under the age of five. I wanted a boat to sail in, one in which I could take the two older kids along. I went searching for a charter. In Falmouth at MacDougalls boatyard, some forty miles away, I heard of a Wianno Senior for sale at Crosby's in Osterville. I backtracked fifteen miles or so and walked into Crosby's ancient main shed, stating my mission to Doug Higham, the wiry boat carpenter who stepped up the moment I entered.

"Well," said he, "we haven't got one for charter, far as I know. 'Course you can ask Bill Crosby, up in the office."

I started up a narrow stair.

"You wanna' buy a boat?"

I came back.

"There's a Senior out there, sitting on the mooring.

Just rebuilt her myself. New keel, new garboards, sheers, new deck—she's all new from the gunwales up. Ask Bill if she isn't good."

I did. Bill said he thought the boat was good as new. And he did not know of any boats for charter.

The next day I was on the way out to the mooring in Crosby's workboat for a trial sail. Innocent of the ways of these gaff-riggers, I had some amusing problems rigging; at least I assume they were amusing to the guys in the boat-yard. On the second try, I got the quadrilateral main on right side up. The wind was light north, dead behind me as I jibed under the drawbridge (giving myself half a scare, the space being narrow, the boom long) and ran down the channel. The boat seemed to sail herself, steady and pleasing in her motion.

I had not been sailing long in the sound when another Senior came close, a man and a woman aboard.

"Want to race?" (Baseball cap. Anxious for a chance to pace with another boat.)

"Oh, I dunno. I'm kind of new at it. Trying her out."

"Well, if she can beat this boat, that'll be going some. This one's won the last seventeen races straight."

So I brought the rebuilt fifty-year-old boat close-hauled for a brush. No cigar. She would foot but not point with them. After three tries, they broke off.

By now we were a mile upwind.

"Try it downwind?" called I.

We sailed side by side in very light air, with little to choose between boats. Finally I slid over directly astern. I eased everything off and sat still.

Slowly the older Senior started riding up the other's stern. Before long, I angled onto his wind and sailed quite rapidly by. Wordlessly, the champion broke off and headed out into the sound.

It was late afternoon, and my boat had picked me.

The next day the fleet champion had his boat hauled—perhaps looking for a flaw? And he did find Higham and asked if all the ballast weights had been put back into the older boat. The carpenter gave his assurances on that point, he told me later. But the champ was dead right. Two years ago, after many seasons of going quite fast downwind in light air but slowly hobbyhorsing upwind in heavy air with a chop, it occurred to me to count the ballast weights myself. We were 120 pounds short—20 percent of the inside ballast!

I asked the rebuilder-owner if I could take her out again with my family. They all loved the boat as much as I did. She sailed like a dream. Lots of room for the kids with an eight-foot cockpit and a cuddy cabin. Pretty lines. Brightwork aplenty. Teak cockpit sole.

Now came the eternal problem. A thousand hours of labor had gone into the rebuilding. The price lay beyond my grasp. I offered. Too little. Summer was marching past. Resigned, I chartered a Duxbury Duck in Wychmere Harbor. She was a cranky elbow-bumper of a boat; someone had altered her by placing a cuddy where there was room for none. Nonetheless the kids and I sailed her every day. We had fun, but I thought often of the Senior. I heard that a man had bought her, writing a check on the spot for the asking price.

Two years passed. We took a cottage in Brewster near the sailing camp I had attended as a boy. I had heard that the man who bought the Senior lived in Orleans, a neighboring town. I asked around. None of my old sailing acquaintances could help. But at the town cove one dawn a friendly stranger told me he had heard of a Senior moored somewhere in Pleasant Bay and suggested I ask Jim Melcher, who ran a sailing camp over that way.

"Sure," said Jim, "I know the boat. It's in a hidden pond. Here's how you get there."

I found the pond at the end of a 2-mile dirt road. I could never have found it without careful directions. The pond was only 150 yards across, and right in the middle was moored the beautiful white-hulled Senior.

I borrowed a dinghy from the beach and rowed out. She had a new gold-leafed cove stripe to match her gold-leafed quarterboard, and shiny brightwork. The cuddy was neat and stripped of excess gear. Lines were neatly coiled. Somebody cared.

Next afternoon I was waiting on the beach as the new owner, Giles Wanamaker, along with his wife and a couple of grown children, hauled their dinghy up after a sail.

I summoned up nerve and introduced myself, telling of my own experience with the boat.

The owner was polite and seemed interested in talking about his boat. We chatted for a minute and he gave me his name and address before they left.

The following spring I wrote him a note asking that he please let me know if he were ever to consider selling.

Two days later I got a telephone call.

"How did you know I wanted to sell the boat?"

"I didn't."

"Well, it's uncanny. We just last week made up our minds to sell."

"How much do you want?"

He named a figure below what he had paid. While I thought a second or two, he named another figure, lower. And said a new outboard went with the deal.

"I want someone to have it," he said, "who'll care for her."

The following week I was at Arey's Pond boatyard at the appointed hour, checkbook in hand. The boat lay dockside, gleaming white, freshly painted, impeccably varnished.

We sat on a log along a beach road, and I wrote the check. I felt him hesitate.

"Are you sure you want to do this?"

"No," he said. "But my wife does. I caught my foot in the mainsheet during a jibe last fall—pulled me almost out of the boat, the way she saw it. She made me promise to sell."

"I don't want to take it from you like that. Won't you talk to your wife again?"

He looked at me. I thought I saw moisture in his eyes.

"No. I have to sell."

That Christmas, at his request, I sent him the gold-leafed quarterboard from her transom. Each summer, I invited him to sail with us, but he never did. After two or three years they sold their house and moved to Florida.

And the boat, having picked me and arranged the unalterable circumstances of her purchase, shortly thereafter sailed me back to Osterville, her old home, my new one.

13

Varnish and Truth

•

Doing your own boat maintenance provides many pleasures. It gets you out of the house on the first warm spring days. It may bring you down to the water's edge if your boat is stored at a boatyard. There you will meet lots of other boating people, providing a nice chance to chat about the upcoming season and things nautical. If you live where boating continues all year, doing maintenance gives you extra time on the boat, time that can turn out to be as satisfying and full of fun as sailing itself. It also gives you a more intimate knowledge of your boat and how it works. All the while, you save your money.

Of course, you may find it is easier and great fun to write checks to the boatyard as the bills come in. As the rates skyrocket, however, some people have suggested that the eventual function of many yards will be to rent space for the owner to work in, to provide expert advice, technical services, and sophisticated heavy equipment for haulouts, launchings, and those jobs that are too heavy for the individual to tackle.

Some yards will not allow owners to work on stored boats. Others impose restrictions: all work below the gunwales belongs to the yard, and boats whose owners do major maintenance will not be stored inside the sheds. The legality of restrictions is being challenged in some states.

By keeping the boat on your own property, you avoid the problem. But few of us have adequate indoor shelter for our boats. Since certain boats definitely should be stored inside in hard climates, the boat owner would be helped a great deal if more boatyards could find a way to support owner maintenance and still make a fair profit.

Wooden boats belong inside. Rain seeps in, forms pools, and encourages rot and peeling paint and varnish. Sun dries the wood and the planks pull apart. A heated garage is even worse than sun in its effect on wood. A shed with a dirt floor is best. It keeps the earth's moisture near the hull, retarding drying.

Wooden boats are protected by paint and varnish on every outside inch and on most interior surfaces too. Alternate freezing and thawing raises hob with the protective coatings. A wooden boat left in the water all winter suffers marked paint damage. Large flakes of paint peel off because of ice abrasion or temperature contrasts between the warmer water and frigid air acting on a hull soaked with the resulting condensation.

Lashing a canvas or plastic winter cover too tightly over your boat can hurt more than help. One winter our boat-yard built a new shed. All the Seniors in that yard were left exposed when the roof of the old shed was removed.

Varnish and Truth

(With beautiful Cape Cod frugality, it was used to roof the new shed, built to fit exactly under it.) Two boats were covered with canvas by the yard, as they were exposed longer than the others. Ours was one. The first warm spring day—at mid-April school vacation suddenly it was 85°—we came down to find heavy canvas covers pulled tightly over the boat, so tightly, in fact, that little or no fresh air could enter. When my son and I pulled the cover back, the temperature in the cockpit was surely over 100°, and the humidity was 100 percent. The trapped salt moisture in the boat's wood had been forcibly released, steaming the brightwork and paint as in a pressure cooker. At the oak coaming butts especially, vapor had worked under the varnish and raised an ugly, white, puffy blister that covered the blackening wood. I promptly lifted the bad varnish and refinished, but the damage can never be completely undone except by replacing the coamings.

The following winter our boat was at the same yard, still unfortunately stored outside. This time I covered it myself. I created large air holes at each end for ventilation. Having moved to Cape Cod year-round, I checked it weekly. Invariably I found that some of the yard personnel had collapsed the structure I had devised to preserve the air holes and had rewrapped the cover tightly. The yards, even with the most helpful of motives, do make an occasional mistake.

Winter covers must allow for air to pass through. I think the best cover framework I ever saw was built of two-by-fours placed vertically to the ground at the boat's bow and stern. These were lashed firmly to the cradle-ends and to the boat. They were tall enough for the transverse two-by-four connecting them to clear all deck obstacles. A wide canvas was stretched over this frame and firmly tied. Its sides extended to ground level. The resulting shape was that of a pup tent, with full open ends for ventilation. I watched that cover all one winter; it never ripped or chafed. The wooden boat under it looked fine in the spring.

Fiberglass—that is, plastic—boats are, in my opinion, best left uncovered when stored outside. Covers seem to abrade and soil their topsides in the winter winds. Unless the boat has much fine brightwork that needs protection, the cover serves little purpose. Plastic stands the weather well. Surely those who own small plastic sailboats and outboard hulls have proven this in their own backyards. In the spring a rubdown with gelcoat cleaner does the job, except on wood trim, which ought to be treated as on a wooden boat.

When spring comes, you can fit your maintenance chores to your skills and your pocketbook. Do what you can; enlist the boatyard for the rest. The people at the yard are the best source of advice on materials and techniques. Nothing can match their experience, their presence on the spot, their knowledge of local boat types and what works in local conditions. If you buy your materials at the yard shop and have the yard do the launching, hauling, and more remunerative jobs, they are repaid adequately for their advice. Usually they are glad to offer it. But be brief and listen carefully. Your conversation time may be charged to some other owner at a fancy hourly rate, but tomorrow it may be turnabout!

In each yard you will find certain people from whom you receive clear answers that prove valuable. Other advice will seem unclear or will not pan out. The solution is obvious. The painter whose advice does not work for you may be the next guy's guru.

Plenty of books cover maintenance procedures. I have not found many as helpful as talking with knowledgeable boatyard people. But you do need a starting point, and a good book will serve if a yard is not available.

Finally, your growing experience will improve your work more than advice from any source. Like the yard, you will make mistakes. As elsewhere, mistakes are your best teachers.

I hope it will be helpful to touch on some of my own mistakes. The first time I varnished (except for Whaler seats and such), I chose a hot, brilliantly sunny day. We had a lot to cover and so kept working through the noontime sun. My older daughter, Deb, then sixteen, helped. I wrongly instructed her to lay it on as thickly as possible without causing it to run. A better suggestion would have been as thinly as possible and still have it cover. Especially on vertical surfaces, and especially for Deb, who by nature likes to glop it on. There are gloppers and go-lighters; you must learn to adjust your suggestions to suit.

Our thick varnish baked in the noonday sun. It dried all too quickly into interesting wrinkles and ridges, my introduction to "alligators" and "lace curtains." I had to scrape down, sand, and start over on another day. Deb pleaded a previous engagement.

That day we had tied the boat alongside the club dock to work. It was late June, the boat had gone in the water weeks before and still was not varnished (another mistake). Just as we finished the last touches, an entire class of ten-year-olds debarked from their Beetlecats onto a nearby float. One splashed water at his friend; another did a picturesque cannonball at perilously close range. My temper sputtered, and I interrupted an enterprising plan to start a waterbomb war. But we now had waterspots decorating our alligators and lace curtains!

For years I had pretty good luck with Sigmavar, a Danish synthetic varnish. About two years ago I began to raise hundreds of tiny air bubbles the size of BB shot. I switched to Z-Spar Captain's varnish. The bubbles continued. I talked to the boatyard paint crew. Nothing helped. Finally I discovered that I had developed a habit of removing excess varnish from the brush by sliding it against the lip of the bucket. That leaves little bubbles in the pooled liquid. The next brushload picks them up, and they puff up on the finished surface in great profusion.

While wooding down brightwork and painted surfaces, I have sometimes leaned too hard on the scraper because it was not sharp enough. It then makes a deep scratch or lifts the grain of the wood, not easy damages to repair. Keeping a file handy and using it often will give you a sharp scraper.

I have varnished on very humid days. The finish comes out duller than you would like. Good varnishers have told me that they always try to varnish first thing in the morning on a dry day. I have found they are right. Varnishing outside after midafternoon is asking for trouble.

I once finished up painting the deck in the evening after supper. We had had a rainy spring, and I wanted to get the boat in the water without further delay. All that season I sailed with certain sections of the deck, the "evening" ones, a mottled, dull version of the intended color. Evening dew does nothing for drying paint. I hate to think what it does to varnish.

I have, of course, made other mistakes. But, mercifully, I cannot recall them all at once. That is perhaps just as well for us both. You will learn from yours—and accumulate maintenance wisdom—better than from anyone else's.

·14·

Race, Anyone?

·

If you keep on sailing, sooner or later someone will ask you to race. The question is, should you?

The answer, I think, derives from human nature as well as cultural factors. Almost all people enjoy races and other competitive sports. But there are differences. The children of a certain American Indian tribe always crossed the finish line of a footrace together; the swiftest simply waited for the slower children to catch up. In spirit everyone won just by participating. This seems to me a lovely way to express and reinforce a spirit of community. It is not often found, however, in present-day sailboat racing. The racing bug that bites us seems to induce a fever which sometimes rises pretty high, a fever to win in the strict sense of placing first. Winners in our society do not often wait around after they have crossed the finish line to greet the losers! So if the bug bites, watch your temperature.

The scene plays something like this: you are sailing along in fine style, content with the peaceful pleasures of the day, when in the corner of your eye you see another boat, same class as yours perhaps, on the same course, not far away. You have to be a very saintly person indeed not to notice which boat goes faster. Next minute you are tinkering a little to try to improve your boat's performance. The racing bug is tickling; soon comes the sting.

Racing, we hope, improves the breed, both of sailors and boats. It is fun too, whether you win, or come in second, or just place high in a competitive fleet. Losing, on the other hand, is said to be good for your character and technically instructive. This is good news, because in racing fleets numbering twenty or thirty and more, only one boat can win each event, and not everyone sails as well as he might. We must conclude that an awful lot of character building and self-education takes place in the remainder of the fleet!

You *can* get hooked so hard on racing that you almost never take your boat out to sail except to race or to practice racing. Since racing effectively demands the highest concentration on a great array of technical details, you will probably forget to enjoy the sun, sea, and sky. That is a pity. The evolution of the racing sailor, we hope, will not end in a mutation blind to the beauty of peaceful pleasures.

Speaking of improving the breed, one wonders if the notion is a tautology self-serving the racing ranks. What breed are we improving? The speed breed—ever quickening the pace around the buoys but taking lightly such essentials as safety, good seamanship, and fair sailing? Sometimes that seems to be the case.

We might as well admit up front the early speedgreed connection. The first yacht races were often challenges sailed for large cash wagers and perhaps the hope of increased business for the winning country's shipping industry. In fact, the *America*'s owners so hoped to lighten their British counterparts' coffers that they left instructions for her to be sailed slowly on her initial appearance in 1851 off Cowes in order to entice larger bets. Sailor's pride got the better of wily planning, however. In their first brush with the English, the *America*'s captain and crew, including one of the owners who was aboard, could not resist the noble impulse to do their best. They sailed so fast that thousands of pounds of potential improvement in the younger country's balance of payments was skittered away. This discomfitted some of *America*'s other owners, who nonetheless subsequently won a nice, big, bottomless Cup, through which millions of units of many national currencies have since figuratively flowed, redistributing big chunks of the western world's wealth from the very rich to the skilled sailmakers, boat builders, designers, and equipment makers, some of whom may well have started out in life poor and worthy. Certain of the big spenders from abroad have reaped immense free advertising in the rich American marketplace by challenging for the Cup; an English tea purveyor, an Australian real estate entrepreneur, a French pen and shaver manufacturer. The speed-money connection works in its own calculating ways.

When you think about it, probably every hard-driving captain, from the early Phoenicians to the Cape Codders pressing every ounce of speed from their clipper ships, had market conditions in mind. The crew may have had other ideas. Not for nothing were those wide sails that billowed from the extended lower yardarms called studding sails.

As presently constituted, however, most sailboat racing involves outlays of money ranging from outrageous to gargantuan with minuscule returns. Cash prizes are few and rarely are side bets substantial enough to qualify as a return on investment. We are looking at pride here and perhaps a search for pure excellence and a little glory as well.

The sport currently has very little commercial sponsorship. Some European newspapers offer prizes for various transoceanic races. A beer company has helped on occasion by quietly sponsoring some United States racing. Professional racing may be on the near horizon, however. At present the hot sail lofts and design offices are exerting a lot of factory team effort, a la Grand Prix auto racing, to produce winners for the big spenders. It brings business. And of course the professionals argue, quite rightly, that the best improvements in equipment eventually spread. Not always, though. Paradoxically, sometimes marvelous innovations are outlawed because, it would seem, they threaten the value of heavy investments already made by owners who carry clout in the rule-making bodies.

And so the reasons for wishing to make boats move more quickly get curiouser and curiouser. But the wish does exist and seems to affect almost all of us if we are scratched deeply enough. Still it may not hurt to bear in mind that a species of superdedicated speed specialists may not be the most desirable end result.

For many small-boat sailors, the positive results of racing will outweigh the negative. Real advances occur in your knowledge of how the boat works, what makes it go, how to handle it in various situations. You study the wind with a much closer eye. You note and use minor shifts that a cruising sailor might leave unmarked. Weather becomes a close companion of your thoughts; you notice it carefully and you try hard to learn its patterns.

Racing is athletic. Pre-Olympic sailors now do body-building exercises that compare with those in other sports. Hiking boards, weight-training programs, jogging, and other disciplines are used to build the needed strengths. Agility and balance are important. Endurance is essential. Class boat racing at the higher levels can involve several consecutive eight-hour days of constant competition.

In offshore boats this turns into days and nights on end. A high level of prolonged concentrated effort is called for. In storm conditions your mental and physical energies may have to be devoted not only to the competition but to saving your life or your companions or the boat, all possibly at risk.

Racing requires thought. It compares to playing chess while doing gymnastics on a tilted, moving platform under a cold shower. You need to think, and think calmly, in these conditions, under extreme time-pressure.

On the other hand, you get a tan, plenty of exercise, and lots of outdoor air.

Racing is social. You will meet other sailors, talk, compare notes, share common experiences. And postrace cocktail parties, awards ceremonies, meetings, dinners, and dances are part of the fun, affording further chances to enjoy your colleagues' company.

On a personal level racing at every stage challenges you to do your best. When you do improve, you feel a growing satisfaction. The real fun may not come until the excitement of your first wins and high places, but the satisfaction of achievement starts early. With it comes increased self-esteem as a sailor and a person. Just measuring up to the peer group, not necessarily winning, will nourish the spirit of almost every beginner. The inexperienced racer probably has the most to gain of any in terms of quantum leaps in his feelings, knowledge, and skills.

Every racing sailor has tales of races won or lost. The longer, more pathetic stories detail the losses. A listener, no matter how attentive, may have difficulty deriving the applicable lesson. I will spare you my racing tales in trust that you will go out and start working on your own.

I do recommend racing to you. But please do not go overboard. Some days are meant just for the pleasures of sailing, at peace and at one with the natural world around you. They are all too easy to give up and very hard to replace.

·15·

Racing Hints for a Beginner

•

This chapter's subject might cause anyone familiar with my current racing record to raise an eyebrow. People who have beaten me regularly and grandly in recent years (almost everybody) may wonder if I am out of my depth. Of course, now that son Steve skippers the Senior, the record looks better. I am occasionally crew, fiddling in the cockpit or wrestling manfully on the foredeck, trying to pass the time gainfully and not distract the skipper. Perhaps I should make this a crew piece.

Most recently I have taken to racing against the kids and a handful of adults in the weekend morning Beetlecat series or, more rarely, in Lasers. After nearly half a century, I find myself back in really small, small boats. And these eleven- to eighteen-year-olds can show you a thing or two!

At least six of our group have won regional championships. Several others have records equally outstanding. They will soon have you talking to yourself on the race course.

Once upon a time, when I was in that age range, luck smiled on me. During some summers wins in almost every race our little camp fleet sailed went to me and Gus Leinbach and Danny Byrnes—two crew as good as any I have ever sailed with. It seemed that, on our home grounds in our local boats, we could hardly lose, even to the occasional hot Edgartown Regatta winner who might drop in.

As a college freshman I brought to the team tryouts only my unsophisticated Cape camp experience. At the end of a long, light day in dinghies I found myself on the four-man Yale sailing team. The other three people were Bob Coulson of Marblehead, one of the few double Sears Cup winners in the history of the sport; Bobby Monetti, a Manhasset, Long Island, light-air genius who ranked in almost every way with Coulson; and Dick Carter, who went on to win the Fastnet twice in boats of his own design, among other world-class yachting achievements. Carter crewed for Monetti, I for Coulson. From these three sailors I began to see how little I knew of racing. Largely through their talents the team won two national intercollegiate titles in four years.

In midcollege years I took off for the Middle East, spending part of 1948 and most of the 1949-50 school year there. I missed two sailing seasons entirely. The team did not seem critically hurt. When Coulson was graduated, Carter stepped in as B skipper and with Monetti won the nationals a second time. Prior to many of these heroics, I had pulled up the board too soon on one of Coulson's artistically hairy mark roundings, and he had enlisted another crew—one who had a better grasp of the phrase "not until I tell you."

Then came graduation, the trek west as a journalist-for-hire, two years with a midwestern daily, time in the backroom mines on Wall Street, and then a family business in Massachusetts to run. During that period I raced a sailboat only once, on a lake in central Massachusetts, and was nonplussed to find that whatever touch I had had in small boats had gone with the wind.

Finally, twenty years out of dinghies, a friend asked if I would help crew their lovely forty-four-foot cutter in an early spring race on Long Island Sound. The boat had been going badly for years, and his father, having visions of better days ahead, had recruited a hot skipper and crew. Two-thirds of the way down the first leg, a long, light air run, however, we were doing so badly that with somewhat desperate hope the helm was turned over to me. I had been cruising in larger boats for the preceding few years, not racing. I had never felt a sweeter-feeling helm than this boat's. She just wanted to go, and with good fortune we began to pick up boats. At the leeward mark we rounded just behind the pack. On the beat the wind freshened. We climbed through the fleet and finally drew even with *Chee Chee IV*. My friend was jumping with joy. All his sailing life his father had wanted to beat—or maybe just get close to—*Chee Chee IV*. Then the genny blew out. The number two went up. The main blew. Good-bye *Chee Chee*. Good-bye glory.

When I got our Senior, my latent racing virus was force-fed by the skipper of a sister boat on the mooring next to ours. He was seeking a boat he could take points from perhaps. After twenty-five years I finally came back to racing.

Such are my modest credentials, and it seems plain I should not be giving exhaustive advice, "inside" tips on racing. Plenty of books do, on many levels of experience. What I would like to offer are a few random hints for the sailor thinking of trying his racing luck.

Race at your own level if possible. Getting horizoned by a more expert fleet is a slow, painful way to learn. In fact, you do not learn when you are too far back of the pack, but you do normally get discouraged.

Get good crew. Appreciate the crew factor. Racing is a team sport if the boat holds more than one. Sailing teams win, not skippers, just as football teams win, not quarterbacks.

Sail. Sail a lot. Practice a lot too: mark roundings, timed starts, spinnaker sets and takedowns, tacks, jibes, the whole gamut. It is satisfying to do, and it should pay off on the race course.

Get the best equipment you can. Then forget it as a factor in the race. Equipment does not win sailboat races in one-design classes, where you will likely be starting out. People do.

If your boat goes slowly, do not accept that as intrinsic to the boat. More likely, the causes lie in your setup and tuning.

Most important, do not let the other sailor convince you he owns a faster boat. This is unlikely in a one-design class. It is important psychologically for you to resist the very idea. He may have faster sails in given conditions, or more likely, set them better, or do a number of things which give his hull superior speed. You can do these things. If you do them better, your hull will go faster.

Learn wind shifts. Use them until doing so is second nature. More races are won in this way than in any other, including pure skill in boat handling.

Racing Hints for a Beginner

If tide is a factor in your area and especially if the race legs are long, study the local tide. Unfortunately, you may need years to unravel local mysteries that are plain to your competitors, but unravel them you must.

Spend money chiefly on sails. They are your engines, and you are in a speed contest. Learn to set sails. Experiment. Pace against another boat, switching one sail, one control, at a time. Get a good sailmaker from the loft to sail with you when you buy a sail. Buy sails slowly, thoughtfully, but do buy them.

Tune your boat. Know your boat. Shroud tension, headstay tension—vary them and note the effects in different wind speeds. Simplify and effectively place your gear. Mast bend, rake, and placement all bear on the sails' ability to supply power. Experiment here too. Install your cleats, cams, leads, winches yourself. No one at the yard can have your feel for their exact placement. Seconds gained in trimming lines translate into feet ahead.

On the race course watch the pattern of the boats on the "chessboard." Keep in mind that you are not racing the clock to the mark but the other boats. Find the front pivot point of the fleet going upwind, get on it if you can, and try to stay on it through all the windshifts and tactical moves.

Start in first or at least up front in the fleet. No matter what your boat speed, you can do this, as starts are primarily made against the clock.

Read racing books that speak to your level of experience, not above, not below. Sail, sail, sail. If you race with poor results, go out and just sail some more.

Have fun doing it! If you do not, return to pure pleasure sailing.

A No-Sail Day

•

A hot, calm day. Noontime and still no breeze. The water in West Bay is smooth. Only the old wake of an occasional powerboat bulges in the placid water. Even the tide has gone slack, dead low. No rips can be seen around the pilings and channel buoys, where on the flood and ebb the current presses. The water is midsummer warm, the sun not strong enough through the haze of the day to heat up the land rapidly. No sign of a thermal nor of a new weather front. The night has been hot, airless. A good day to go touring and swimming.

I get a bathing suit and old beach towel from the back of the car. Steve is somewhere around, perhaps at Crosby's snack bar having lunch with the other yacht club instructors. He will not want the Whaler. Deb is a college

junior working as a swimming teacher in East Hampton
for the summer. Mark, a freshman-to-be, is a municipal
lifeguard in the central part of the state, living at his
mother's house for the summer, as is Polly, our youngest,
who is practicing daily with her swimming team. I have no
lessons to give this airless day, and boat maintenance is
pretty well caught up now that it is early August. The
Whaler—and time—are my own.

I propose to take a tour around the adjoining bays—
an interconnected waterway of unusual scope and beauty.
I will beach the boat, lie in the sun, and swim when the
fancy strikes me. I know of plenty of places along the way,
some hidden so well that they become for the time one's
own private coves and beaches.

I hop in the Whaler from the float on the dock, cast off
painter and stern-line clip, and start up the engine. With the
throttle just past idle, I swing slowly out through the
mooring basin in the wide shallows of upper West Bay.
Some people call this particular section South Bay. It lies
mostly east and north of the main body of West Bay,
connected by a broad opening between Garrison's and
Wright's Points. It is south of North Bay, but on grounds
that south should not lie northeast of west, I shall go on
calling it part of West Bay. Perhaps a hundred sailboats
moor here in one to seven feet of water. They range from
twelve-foot Beetlecats to forty-four-foot sailing auxiliaries.

I soon arrive at the far end of the mooring area, about
two hundred yards from the dock, near the eastern shore
where our Senior lies. I check the boat to see that all looks
well. It does. I resist the temptation to go aboard, knowing
that if I do, I will putter and fix and straighten up until half
the day slips by.

The Whaler's blunt nose is turned west toward the
channel. Eel River is southward, a quarter mile long, only

about fifty feet wide, with shoal along its banks, but it is deep enough in midchannel for a Bermuda 40 and a large white Hinckley yawl. Both boats are tied alongside docks in front of their owners' houses, which are set well back from Eel River. This is a nicer place than its name conveys. Several boathouses and many docks line the water's edge. Only a one-hundred-yard wide sandy neck with a road across a causeway separates the end of the river from Nantucket Sound. Oldtimers say that, one day, a southeast storm at the flood will break through here and isolate the big houses on the mile-long Wianno point at the outer end of Sea View Avenue. Perhaps, though it did not happen in the great storm of February, 1978. Since it dead-ends so abruptly, I rarely go up Eel River. Today I pass its entrance by.

I often stand when steering a stable skiff or Whaler. So do fishermen and boatyard workers in their sturdy workboats. You can see better, move about faster, and cushion wave shocks more comfortably. Easily capsized boats—dinghies, canoes, shells, some boardboats and small sailboats—present a tricky platform for standing. So we normally ask beginners to sit down, equating sitting with safety. Having learned this lesson, people continue to sit down in larger boats that are difficult to capsize with the weight of several persons standing on the gunwale. If the boat has initial stability, standing is just as safe and perhaps safer. I hold onto the painter or the stern line, or the wheel or tiller, for balance. In large boats, the helmsman rarely sits down unless the boat is on a very easy, problem-free course. On ships, theoretically, never.

Inexperienced passengers, on the other hand, should probably be seated. They often lack a handhold and cannot anticipate which way, or how suddenly, the boat will move. The helmsman can see better if they sit too.

In our Whaler I often remove the aft thwart, where the driver normally sits, to make better standing room. On straightaways I steer at low speed either by shifting weight from side to side or guiding the wheel, which is too low to reach otherwise, with my lower leg. The sensation is something like that of skiing gently down an easy slope. It is pleasant; I commend it to those with the proper boats.

So, standing in the Whaler and steering with my leg, I pass at slow speed between Wright's and Garrison's Points into the wider, larger part of West Bay. On my right hand, between Wright's Point and the windmill at Oyster Harbors gatehouse, lies the sandy southern shore of Little Island. At the end of this thousand-yard stretch—along which some ten or twelve summer houses front—lies a little cove with only a foot or so of water at low tide. It extends almost to the windmill. Its banks are lined with eel grass higher than the water is deep. Two summer houses snugly hide in the pine groves along its shore.

This little cove is separated from North Bay by a causeway to Grand Island. I could throw a stone into North Bay from here, but traveling by water I will have to go over three miles around Grand Island to reach the place where it would fall.

Going out of the cove and down West Bay, which is about a half mile wide, the high bank along the eastern shore of Grand Island is on my right. Water depths between the midbay channel and the shore are only one to three feet at this tide, though subchannels lie near the shore. Along the Grand Island bluffs, about a half-mile stretch, is another line of about ten large summer homes. The last group of four houses sits along the little peninsula that juts into the junction of the Bay, the Seapuit River, the cut, and Mellon's cove.

On the left, past Garrison's Point, lies the western

sandy shore of Wianno. Set back on high ground are five or so large homes. Toward the mouth of the channel the water on the bay's east side thins out in places to three or four inches, though you can find a six-foot-deep subchannel by the shore. Here the tip of Wianno right-angles back toward the center of the bay, almost enclosing its southern end. The land here is lower, with houses along the beach. The last house looks across the two-hundred-yard gap at the mouth of West Bay and down the Seapuit River.

As the Whaler slides through the bay's end, I have several choices. By turning right I can follow the narrow Seapuit River, which is really not a river but a saltwater connector from West to Cotuit Bays, a sort of inland waterway. It divides the southern sandy shore of Grand Island from a thin island-dune known as Dead Neck or—at its Cotuit Bay extremity—Sampson's Island.

If I go straight out through the Osterville cut into Nantucket Sound, I can proceed around the outside of Dead Neck/Sampson's Island and reenter the bay system at Cotuit. I can beach the boat and swim on either side of Sampson's. The Audubon Society has managed the fragile island-dune since the donation of the land as a bird sanctuary by residents of Grand Island. Access is limited to local residents and society members holding permits. The bird population consists chiefly of sea gulls.

I turn into the Seapuit River. The hot afternoon has brought picnickers and swimmers to Dead Neck. Their boats are anchored or beached. To the right is the south side of Grand Island, an island that, when I finally return to West Bay, will have been circumnavigated, as will Little Island. Along the Grand Island shore are more houses, about fifteen in the mile-long stretch. There are several solidly built docks with solidly built boats tied to them.

A No-Sail Day

The sea gulls across the river—which is only thirty-five yards wide at low tide and ten more at high—nest and chatter and hatch their young in a somewhat more raucous manner than their neighbors on the other side, the donors of the sanctuary. The benefactors have benefited themselves, not entirely accidentally perhaps, by limiting the beach traffic opposite their homes, protecting from overuse a natural barrier for their beachfronts, and removing the property from both the tax rolls and the reach of possibly unwelcome purchase.

On breezy days it is fun to sail through the Seapuit. The southwest wind comes with full force over Dead Neck, heeling your boat, but the water remains smooth as a rippled pond, protected from the waves by the barrier of the dune. Today, breezeless, even the normally cool Whaler floor feels hot to bare feet. I begin to think of a swim. I throttle up a little, though the Seapuit has a six-mile-an-hour limit. Emerging from the river, I cross the southeastern corner of Cotuit Bay. I double back through Cotuit cut around the outside of Sampson's Island. After a few hundred yards I anchor and step off onto the outer beach of Sampson's.

Not a person is in sight. Heat waves shimmer off the sand, too hot to walk on barefoot. I move up the beach quickly to a hollow in the dunes and sunbathe. Soon, perspiring, I run for the water and dive in. The drop-off here is steep—ten feet from shore the water is over my head—which is not true of any but this stretch of the Sampson's beach. The water is about 70°, pleasingly cooler than the air, which must be 100° just above the sun-heated sand. The swimming is good.

After an hour of swimming and sunbathing, I climb wet, cooled, and happy into the Whaler, towel off my face, and resume my tour. The channel crooks back around

Sampson's through Cotuit cut, bends the other way past Bluff Point—one house on its height and several newer ones on the slope nearer the beach—and then into Cotuit Bay. At 1¾ miles, Cotuit Bay is longer than West Bay and a little wider. The village of Cotuit sits on its western shore; a lovely church spire, a few houses, the town dock visible through the masts of about a hundred moored sailboats.

The water in midbay is as much as sixteen to twenty feet deep, far deeper than West Bay, deep enough so that in the late 1800s and early 1900s coastwise schooners came through Cotuit Bay and sailed around as far as Osterville landing near the foot of Bay Street, there to unload cargoes of coal and bulk goods. On their right hand was a forested Grand Island, prior to that known as Hannah Screechum Island after Captain Kidd's Indian consort. He murdered her and buried her body on the island so her ghost would protect the hiding place of his pirate treasure. Nowadays the island's shore shows glimpses of summer homes set among the trees, and it is beach-lined. On the Cotuit shore opposite, one sees houses, also generously spaced; a village beach with more sailboats moored off; and, as the bay sides begin to close in, the low gray shacks of the Cotuit Oyster Company, whose outboard-powered barge drags the most delicious oysters out of its grant beds in the bay shallows. Here too is a mooring area of perhaps thirty small boats, mostly sail.

In Cotuit and North Bays during World War II the army engineers and Coast Guard trained amphibious landing craft operators for D day and the Pacific landings. Two camps were set up, named with whimsical Cape Cod humor in the spirit of the times: Camp Canduit in North Bay and Camp Havdunit at Crosby's boatyards in Osterville. One Cotuit historian recalls that the beach was blacktopped from the oyster company to the Narrows to facilitate the operation. Practice landings were made on Dead Neck and other beaches further west on Nantucket Sound at Waquoit and Poponesset.

Beyond the oyster company for the next half mile a passage—the Narrows—leads into North Bay. The schooner skippers bound for Osterville must have needed patience and cunning to sail through. High hills line both banks, between which the gap is only about 150 feet; winds are fluky; the buoyed channel is hardly more than 50 feet wide and 6 feet deep today. It has shoaled some in the intervening years, but can you imagine sailing in here with a 100-foot schooner, engineless, full-laden, and shorthanded?

Passing out of the Narrows, I stay in the marked channel for another 250 yards. A 1-foot shoal lies on either hand at low tide. Then, North Bay, almost a perfect oval, ¾ of a mile long by a ½ mile wide.

Here is the hurricane hole for many of the south shore boats. Some two dozen hollow steel balls about six feet in diameter glower on its surface—hurricane moorings for the larger yachts. Other boats—several hundred came in during the last hurricane scare in 1978—merely anchor within the bay's protection. It is nearly two miles inland from Nantucket Sound. Its shores are sandy, again discreetly lined by houses. At its north end the little Marstons Mill river curves a quarter mile through eel grass banks and hidden marshes to Prince's Cove, a smaller, muddy-bottomed mooring area and storm refuge. Dam Pond, Bog Pond, and Ishem Pond indent North Bay's northeast shore, all but Dam Pond too shoal for navigation except by canoe or skiff. On the opposite side of North Bay a pretty cove extends about five hundred yards to the causeway over which I could have thrown a stone at the trip's start near the Oyster Harbors gatehouse.

North Bay is a designated water-ski area. This afternoon, with no wind and hot sun, two or three skiers are out—a crowd as things go in North Bay. The sport always looks dangerous to me. As a boatman I see some potential for one ski boat in a closed area to hit another at high speed while both drivers are distracted by the business and excitement of towing a skier. The rules require each boat to carry a second person as observer to discourage the driver from looking back, but he looks back anyway at times. The big steel hurricane buoys are a hazard too, as are miscellaneous other boats traversing the bay. I give the kids in the ski boats a wide berth, heading east and then southward into the channel that will take me under the bascule bridge into West Bay.

This channel leads through low-lying land left and right to a boat basin about five hundred yards long. Almost everywhere it is lined by the docks and slips of the two Crosby yards. In the middle of this basin, which is about two hundred yards wide and is often called simply "the river," are moored some large sailing auxiliaries. Power boats are slipped alongside the docks. The two boatyards are a source of never-ending interest, providing a seasonal spectacle of comings and goings, of big boats and small, local boats and occasional visitors from far ports, spring launchings and fall haulouts, and the painting, repairing, carpentry, rigging, and plain ingenuity that go into caring for the boats. Many older, quite beautiful wooden boats still sail from here, as do reinforced plastic and metal boats. Wooden boats are still built and rebuilt in the Crosby sheds as craftily as ever. Plastic hulls are sometimes built or finished out nicely in wood. The nature and expertness of the work done at both yards commands attention. The first Crosbys started to build boats along these shores in about

1800. The boats they built are known and respected throughout the sailing world.

Just past the Crosbys the river narrows to sixty feet and flows beneath the bascule bridge. I pass under its twenty-one-foot central span into West Bay against a flooding tide that sluices around the pilings. On the right bank is Joe Crosby's quite picturesque oyster shack. Several fishing skiffs are tied up in front. Then Wright's Point again, and opposite, on the left bank, the club dock.

I tie up the Whaler. I have motored almost five miles while only once retracing my route, spent three delightful hours, had a swim at an isolated beach—yet just skimmed the surface of these wonderful bays, cuts, rivers, coves, ponds, and channels. It takes many a no-sail day to know them well.

·17·

Sails

.

Sails are so beautiful that analyzing how they work seems altogether unpoetic. Furthermore, even experts disagree on the answers to some questions, and on the emphases on certain factors. The inquiry becomes a chase and puzzle. Most of the carefully thought-out theories do not work especially well when actually applied to building faster sails. Then some sailmaker's error results in the fastest sail in the fleet. The scientists sit down ex post facto to figure out and explain why. Eventually we have a modified, improved, even brilliant theory. Its sanctity lasts until the next fortunate mistake.

Progress may not always happen that way. But it happens often enough so that you can remain healthily skeptical of any theory you read about sails, including what appears in the following paragraphs. Little is known; much is written.

A sail set wide to catch the wind from aft draws force from the push of the wind on the presented side. Or does it?

If the wind is piling up against a wide-set sail's facing surface, it creates higher pressure against that surface than on the back side. The lower atmospheric pressure on the back side must really therefore suck the sail forward. Not, as we first thought, the push on the front surface. Right?

Yes, right, although I am not sure you have said anything very beneficial or uplifting when you have said this. When the pressure increases on one side of the sail, it becomes relatively lower on the other. In a simpler age, we might have been content to ascribe the moving force to the push and ignore the pull.

But this is not a simpler age. For instance, here is an odd fact: bag out a mainsail on a run on a light day, and it will go faster than a flat sail. But, bagged (i.e., bellied to maximum curve by easing outhauls, downhaul, other controls), the sail actually presents less surface area for wind to push, since it is not stretched so far on the spars. The boat might be expected to go slower. But it does not.

The nice, curved back side is thought to cause this oddity. Air seeping around the edges of the sail runs clingingly along it like syrup over a pancake. That is the nature of air; it acts like a fluid. After curling around the edges of the sail, it flows along the back side faster than the air that is pooled and slowed in the belly of the baggy sail. Air going faster over one side of a surface creates lower pressure on that side, the physicists tell us. Ergo, more pull and more boat speed.

Finally the air detaches from the back-side curve, delaminates as the flow analysts say, and goes on its hastened way, having pulled—we think—like mad.

The famous example usually given is an airplane wing. Because it is curved on its top surface and flatter on the bottom (you can check next time you fly), a wing lifts. At least so we are told. If that is so, how can stunt planes fly upside down? I can only refer you to the aeronautical engineering books. And remind you about skepticism when confronting an all-encompassing theoretical explanation.

I took as an extreme example the sail set wide for running free. The back-side suction effect may be clearer if we consider a close-hauled sail. Maybe.

The breeze strikes the sail's leading edge at an angle of around thirty-five degrees. (If you are lucky enough to be sailing a Cup defender, at less than thirty degrees, but of course most boats are not so close-winded.) The sail is curved, of course. The depth of the curve—the draft, or chord—can be decreased or increased and moved forward or aft by means of the hauls, by mast bend, boom bend, cutting and sewing of sails, and other means. The breeze divides on the mast and the sail's leading edge. Some goes around back side, some across the front. We learn from current theory that the wind traveling the back-side curve must hurry to catch up with its sister breeze that took the shorter route around front. The higher relative airspeed creates lower pressure on the back side. Suction pull goes to work.

This is pretty well-accepted theory nowadays. It must be generally useful, and I certainly do not want to meddle with well-enough. Did you ever see a cloth sail, or even a mylar one, however, that had a flatter curve in front than in back? The wind on the front follows a concave curve, just as the sister wind around back clings to the matching convex one. Then why would the divided breeze travel at differing speeds over our "wing"? Lives there a sailmaker who can make a cloth sail that will exhibit greater curve on one of its sides?

Hold on a minute. Look at the Chinese box kite: flat, spaced pieces strongly joined by light frames. Flies like a bird. Like an airplane wing. Like a sail. Wins prizes at the kite picnic. And not a curved surface on it.

Maybe the kite's tail gives it flying ability. As a matter of fact, yes. But you figure it out. We have to talk about sails now.

The fact that a back-side low-pressure force is at work on a curved sail may be caused by a slower moving pool of air that fills a close-hauled sail's front-side pocket, somewhat trapped by its saucer shape. In effect, this puddle of air thickens and flattens the shape of the front side. The back-side air *then* has to move faster to catch up. That would create low-pressure suction.

But what about the fellow flying in his upside-down airplane? The curve of his wings bulges toward the ground. The flat side points skyward. According to our theory, he should be plummeting to earth since his wing's lift is working in reverse.

Back to the drawing board. Newton's third law holds that for every action, there is an equal and opposite reaction. When the wind blowing in a given direction strikes a sail, it is forced to change its direction. The reaction to this change is equal and opposite: the sail tries to move the boat in the direction opposite to that of the wind's change. The boat's underbody converts this sideways thrust into forward motion. In my opinion this is the chief force acting to drive a sail forward.

We must still give fair credit to back-side suction,

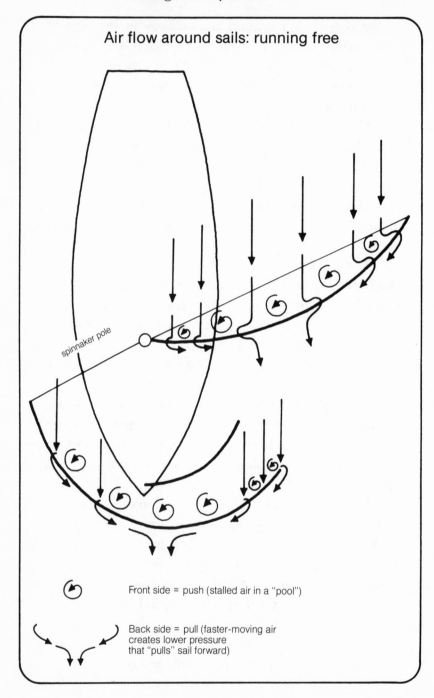

Air flow around sails: running free

spinnaker pole

Front side = push (stalled air in a "pool")

Back side = pull (faster-moving air
creates lower pressure
that "pulls" sail forward)

Curvature of sails

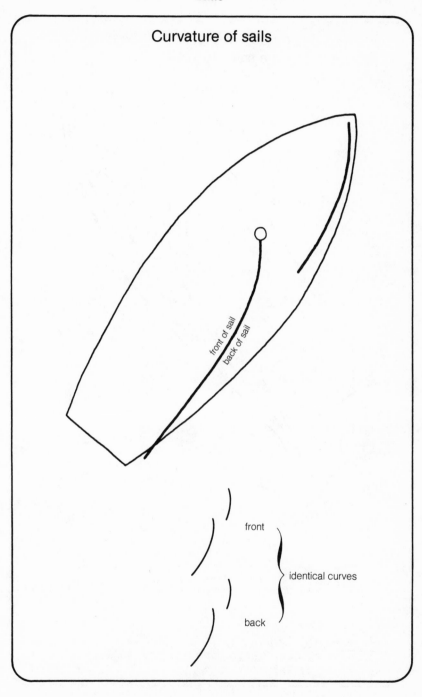

front of sail

back of sail

front

back

identical curves

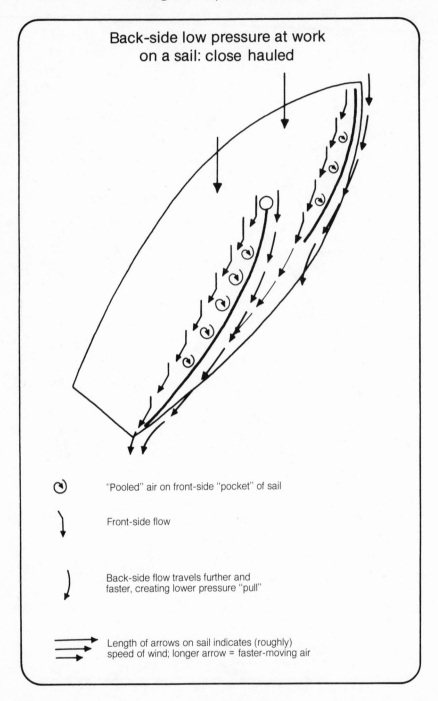

Back-side low pressure at work on a sail: close hauled

"Pooled" air on front-side "pocket" of sail

Front-side flow

Back-side flow travels further and faster, creating lower pressure "pull"

Length of arrows on sail indicates (roughly) speed of wind; longer arrow = faster-moving air

The chief force driving a sail: equal and opposite reaction to change in the wind's course

| | Wind |
| Wind is forced to change direction |
| Produces equal reaction opposite to the bisect of the angle of change |

though I think it contributes less to the vector (quantity and direction of forces acting on the sail) than many sailors believe. In fact, some of the back-side components pull more aft than forward on a close-hauled sail (lower leech), and many pull the sail sideways.

The components that produce a sideways thrust are somewhat converted to forward thrust by the resistance of the boat's underbody and its keel-centerboard-rudder complex. Otherwise sailboats would go largely sideways when close-hauled. Sail close-hauled in a flat-bottomed centerboarder with the board up. You will see how much to the side the vector of the sail can be.

Now perhaps we can ascribe to the wide-set sail, with which we began this chapter, its satisfactory component forces. It would seem to push and pull straight downwind if the sail is set properly. The chief force is push—a reaction to the blocking of the wind's free passage. The back-side pull provides a small increment in the strength of the vector and no change in this case in its direction. But as racers well know, the small increment is not too small to help produce a victory if rightly courted.

We have not discussed the forces on sails while on a reach. I believe you can extrapolate. No one knows all the answers. You may come up with something new and reach faster and better than us all.

We also have not discussed apparent wind, a result of the boat's forward motion. Put your hand out of a moving car's window on a windless day. You feel artificial wind: wind created by the motion of the vehicle. Its direction is always from forward of the natural wind, since artificial wind must by definition come from dead ahead. It modifies the angle of natural wind, bringing the direction of the combined winds—the so-called apparent wind—slightly forward. The apparent wind denotes the direction of the

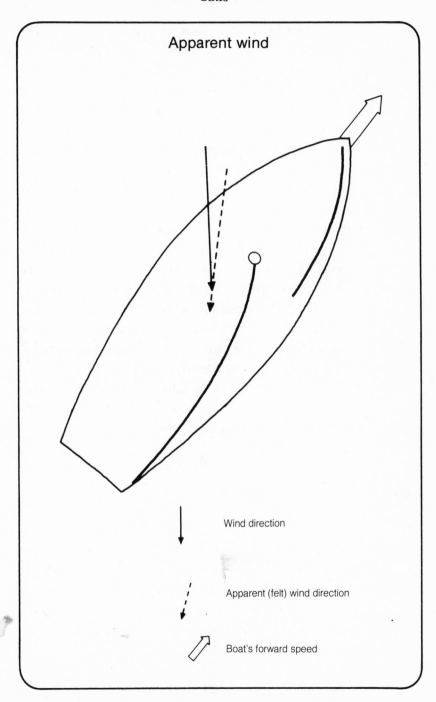

Apparent wind

Wind direction

Apparent (felt) wind direction

Boat's forward speed

felt wind as it strikes you or your sail, taking into account the boat's forward speed. The sail will act as if a little closer to the wind than you would have expected—or quite a lot closer if your boat is a fast one. It is useful to bear that in mind, but it does not change the basic nature of the forces driving a sail.

We also have not peered into the nooks and crannies of much sail lore, all the way from the drag of tight leeches to the efficiency of the Chinese junk rig. But hold on; we have to stop somewhere.

Before we do, let's go back to see if we can settle what keeps the upside-down airplane flying. Suppose the pilot keeps the plane's nose up. The force of the reaction from the wind being redirected by the upward-angled under-side of the wing (the angle of incidence) should hold the plane aloft despite the curve on the wing's underside. The wing does not lift as efficiently as one right side up. Nor can the plane fly as fast. But it does fly.

So does the Chinese box kite, whose tail's weight angles its leading-edge surfaces upwards, allowing the breeze to strike the underside, where its change of direction produces lift.

Now about a perfectly flat sail. . . .

18

Wind and Calm

·

One summer morning you arrive at the dock early. Sea gulls are sitting placidly on the pilings. The water is flat. Mooring lines sag. Nearby boats point in opposite directions; the tide has divided into a main stream and a back current. No wind.

Do you go sailing? Will wind come up later? The weather forecast will not really help you decide; it is not very accurate for local wind conditions.

The thing to do on a hot, sunny day in summer is wait. Periods of flat calm do not often last long in summer in our area. Where water and land adjoin, the temperature difference between the sun-heated land and the more temperature-stable water causes thermals, rising columns of hot air. When the hotter air over land rises, it sucks in a breeze.

In New England, when the vast forestland of Maine to the northeast starts to heat rapidly under a July sun, the thermal can draw in twenty-five knots of southwest breeze after a morning's dead calm. It will blow from seaward across Nantucket and Martha's Vineyard, cross the twenty-five-mile sound, then travel three or four times that distance over the Cape Cod and Massachusetts bays until it brushes the Maine coast. Finally somewhere inland it starts its upward rise. Even on days when the circulation in a high pressure system adds little impetus, this thermal blows strongly.

Later in summer, haze and low cloud may obscure the sun. Its angle is also lower in the sky. The land will not heat so rapidly. The water has warmed to 70° or more, further cutting the temperature differential. A faint southerly wind may result from a stagnant low pressure system to the southwest. Under these conditions, the thermal may not come in at all or may come less strongly and later in the afternoon.

In any case our local experience tells us that a dead calm will not last longer than an hour or two. That is why I do not give up on the day's sail quite yet.

You will learn to recognize the conditions in your locality that bring a new breeze out of the calm. When it is a half mile or so away, you will see signs of the breeze approaching: dark ripples on the water's mirrored slick, sailboats moving in the distance, flags, clouds. With experience you can predict the time of the wind's arrival fairly accurately. Sharpen your observations and you will also become good at predicting the direction and strength of the new breeze.

Wind and Calm

If you go down to sail and find a dead calm in the afternoon, in our area it is probably the day to catch up on maintenance. Look for signs of a thermal or a new weather front. If you do not see any, start for the locker or the marine store. After all, the sun has had plenty of time to heat up the land. If no breeze has come up yet, the chances do not look good that one will. What you would like now is a high or low pressure system to arrive, bringing within its circulation steady winds. These systems are normally accompanied by major shifts from the preceding wind direction and by a basic change in the weather. Forecasts predict them more accurately than they do local thermals. Sometimes you can step outside and almost feel the change coming.

The systems are several hundred miles in diameter. They are themselves confluences of thermals. Low pressure systems form when masses of warm southern air rise; in this hemisphere, air in low pressure systems moves in a counter-clockwise rotation. Warm, rising air lowers atmospheric pressure at ground level—hence, a low pressure system. The whole organized system is borne across the United States in a basically west-to-east upper air flow, sometimes curving and dipping north and south. The lows tend to travel north and eastward from southern warmth; the highs south and eastward from Canadian cool. The winds we feel as part of a low pressure system carry clouds and often precipitation, since the moisture in warm air rises high enough to cool and condense it in the upper atmosphere; this condensed moisture returns to earth as rain.

Cold, heavy air eventually falls back to earth, raising atmospheric pressure at the surface and forming a high pressure cell. This air is relatively devoid of moisture, and

Typical track of Canadian high pressure system

Formation of high pressure cell; arrow indicates direction of winds within system

High pressure cell approaches New England: northwest winds

High pressure cell south of New England: west winds

High pressure cell southeast of New England: southwest winds

Typical Canadian high pressure system track

cP   Canadian polar (cold) air

in descending it warms and dries out further. High pressure systems rotate clockwise in this hemisphere. The highs contain clear, dry, crisp air. They will bring first northwest, then west, and finally southwest winds if the center of rotation passes to the south of you, as it often does in New England.

The pressure systems are the huge factories of weather and wind. When they and the local thermals are both stagnant, it is a rare day in our area. A calm one. Not for sailing.

If you are caught out on the water in a breeze that drops dead, relax and enjoy the interlude. Lie on deck. Watch how the tide or current moves your boat—it will be useful information in the future, especially if you race in these waters. Look at the sails hanging still against the sky. You will remember some of these quiet moments with fondness as some of the best in small-boat sailing.

Of course you can trade such moments in for an auxiliary power package: an outboard, gas tank, gas-oil mix, funnel, spare shear pin, battery, extra starter pull cord, and spark plugs. Then you can do what the larger auxiliary cruising sailboat invariably does: start your engine and not only shatter nature's calm but quite possibly your own, either through the noise and fumes when it does start or your frustration when it does not.

If your boat is small enough and you have enough experience to maneuver in crowded harbors without auxiliary power, then leave the engine off. It takes up space, makes noise, uses energy, and deprives you of what nature rarely provides—calm.

19

Tide

·

Here on Nantucket Sound the tide rises and falls as predictably as the moon revolves about the earth. Tide here takes about six hours and ten minutes to come in. And another six hours and ten minutes to go out. One complete cycle takes about twelve hours and twenty-plus minutes. So tomorrow afternoon's high tide will occur about forty to fifty minutes after today's; tide peaks at 1:00 P.M. today, 1:40 P.M. tomorrow, 2:30 P.M. or perhaps 2:40 the third day, and roughly so on.

Tide is strange. At Boston it rises anywhere from eight to twelve feet going from low to high, ebb to flood. The range occurs because of the positions of the moon and sun. Tide height is also affected by passing low pressure systems: low pressure on the water's surface allows the water level to lift; high pressure inhibits it. That is one reason why a storm, which accompanies a low pressure system, presents special flooding problems along the coast.

Tide is not the same around the globe. In the Caribbean Islands the normal rise is about one foot from low to high. Nor does it peak there every twelve-plus hours; in some areas it peaks only once a day. Strangers to the area often cannot tell when high tide occurs, or if the tide has changed at all.

A few hundred miles north of Boston in the Bay of Fundy, where the water enters a wide-mouthed dead-end funnel, the tides at the far end climb fifty feet against the shore. At Inchon, South Korea, forty feet. Along the English Channel's coastline, almost as much. But in the Mediterranean, as in the Carribbean, a foot of tide is hard to find.

Strangely enough, many sailors have an amazing lack of knowledge about the tides. Just last summer a young man I know who has sailed intensively for fourteen years was surprised to find out that the highs and lows come progressively almost an hour later each day in our area. He had not noticed!

Though no oceanographer or nautical meteorologist, I will try to set out a few bits of information about the tides and then quickly get on to talking about how sailors find practical use in them.

The moon's gravitational attraction contributes to the creation of tide. To a lesser extent, so does the sun's. When they both line up so as to exert pull in the same direction, the rise will be higher (twelve feet at Boston, not eight). And the low will be lower. When they line up and pull in opposite directions, the tides will also be extreme. That is because a high tide occurs on opposite sides of the globe simultaneously.

The moon and sun are not the sole gravitational forces

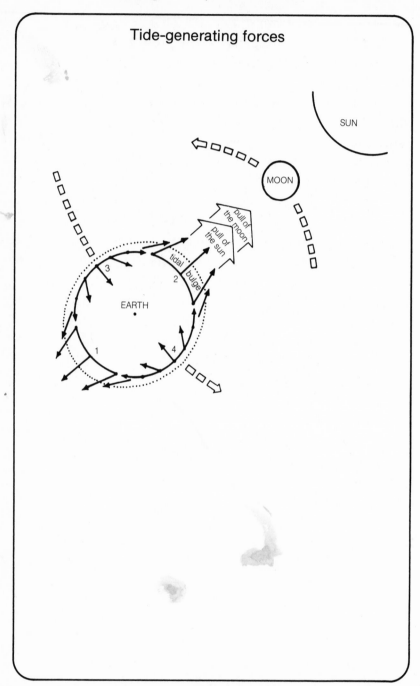

Tide-generating forces

Tide

Tide-Generating Forces

Arrows show various directions and magnitude (proportional to length of arrow) of forces generating tides. The forces involved are: the pull of the moon's gravity, the pull of the sun's gravity, the pull of the earth's gravity (toward its center) and the centrifugal force of rotation. Differences in the balance among these forces acting on given particles of water at various points on earth create the tide.

Note: The *angle* of the pull of the moon's and sun's gravity to that of the centrifugal force of the earth's rotation (around the joint center of gravity of all three bodies) is *nearly the same* on opposite sides of the earth. That is why nearly the same high tides occur simultaneously at points 1 and 2, and of course low tides at points 3 and 4.

affecting ocean waters. The earth's gravity is a far greater force. It pulls directly inward towards earth's center, in opposition to the outward pulls of the sun and moon toward their positions at the moment. The in-pull and the out-pulls occur at different angles to the ocean waters. This creates one component of the side-pull that is the tide-creating force.

This force acts simultaneously at directly opposite points on the globe because centrifugal force—force exerted outward on bodies spinning around a joint center of gravity, in this case, the sun, earth, and moon—is also at work on the surface water. Let us suppose that the gravitational pull when the moon and sun line up together over the South Atlantic exerts itself on a line through the earth to the floor of, in this instance, the China Sea. The angle between the pull and the constant outward force of the centrifuge very nearly equals a similar angle formed on the South Atlantic side of the earth although that side happens to be nearer the source of pull. Thus we have two tides on opposite sides of the globe that rise and fall at the same time in very nearly equal magnitude. The *angles* of the component forces create tide, and these angles are nearly the same on opposite sides of the globe at the same instant.

The rise and fall of tides in open ocean is almost imperceptible. Only when the rising water encounters resistance from underwater topography or immense land barriers does its movement become apparent, being greater or smaller depending on the configurations encountered. Thus the Bay of Fundy's fifty-foot rise and the free-standing small Caribbean Islands' almost invisible one foot of rise.

Tides exist on lakes and inland seas too. The same forces are at work. But, given the minuteness of the component forces creating tide, only the largest bodies of

Tide

water sloshing against the most gigantic land masses produce a noticeable effect.

More can be studied on this subject, but even the basic answers about this seemingly elemental phenomenon are not fully known in this, the atomic age, since we have somewhat neglected the study of the ocean until quite recently.

Clearly the tide holds very little practical interest for the lake sailor. For ocean sailors—and lake sailors who sooner or later will find ocean water under their boats—it is a factor to reckon with. It creates mile-wide flats on the north side of Cape Cod. It shoals West Bay to a one-inch depth where six hours before we sailed in three or four feet of water. It creates tidal currents to be planned for and used by cruising sailors. It swings heavy boats at anchor until they foul less affected lighter boats. It influences race outcomes, wave heights, and for all we know the psychological equilibrium of sailors.

So for ocean sailors, knowing the tide's state is important. Elaborate tables show highs and lows for almost every coastal location in the United States. The tables also show the spread between high and low for each successive tide. In calm conditions the predicted spread will hold. If a powerful wind blows offshore during a receding tide, or vice versa, that tide may well exceed its expected range. An important storm occurring near the time of high tide and having strong onshore winds will add to the tide's height. If a low pressure center passes at the time of an expected peak-range high tide, the resultant flooding and wave pounding may produce a coastal disaster.

Keep your copy of the tide tables handy but also watch for natural signs of the tide. It tilts buoys over in varying degrees; observing this will tell you something about its strength that day. The marks left on the sand as the tide recedes offer a sort of tidal hourglass. So do the watermarks on dock pilings. Where tide sluices around objects, it indicates its direction and velocity by ripples in the water. Surface flotsam and jetsam, sometimes the surface of the water itself, reveal tide movement to the alert eye.

If you know where it is going, you can use the tide. An afternoon's pleasure sail works out well if you lay a course that brings you home with the tide. Keep in mind that waves will not be as steep when wind and tide travel in the same direction. Lay your boat up on the beach at high tide for a free maintenance haulout. Calculate the rise and use it to sail in otherwise unnavigable water. Calculate the fall and avoid temporarily shallow grounds.

The mention of ground brings up the subject of going aground. In shoal, sandy areas such as West Bay a sailor may develop a practiced style of running aground if he is venturesome and new to the area. One way to handle the embarrassment is to stand right up, remove excess clothing, and dive in as if you have made a planned swim-and-luncheon stop. While in the water munching a sandwich, nonchalantly push the boat off. The nonchalance will mark your sailing experience and also help keep your temper down, improving health and life expectancy. Do not forget to push the boat in the direction opposite to the way it went aground. Leave the making of new underwater trenches to the dredging crew.

Of course, in bigger boats, bigger problems. Powerful tows may be needed. Or kedging with anchors, rocking, heeling the boat with halyards, boom-weights— whatever it takes to get her off. Sadly, when a boat goes up on a rocky shore or reef, she may be finished. It depends on the damage at impact and/or the damage from wave action lifting the boat up and smashing it down before she can be freed.

The tide may play a well-hidden part in causing big-boat groundings. Its currents have set navigators far off course when closing a continental coast. In fog, lacking electronic navigational aids, the sailor closing a coastline can be headed for unsuspected trouble, having picked up a red number 6 buoy that is fifty miles from the identically marked buoy he thinks he has sighted. Such are the vagaries of our repetitive coastal buoy marking system. Behind the wrong red number 6 may lie rocks rather than the open water expected.

Keep your eye on the tide. It waits for no man, as we know. But rightly caught, it works for all.

20

The Other Side of the Cape

·

I have often referred to the Nantucket Sound, or the south side of Cape Cod, but seldom to its "other" side. Which side is the other depends of course on where the speaker's loyalties reside. In either case it seems a good idea to pay a visit to the Cape Cod Bay shore, which stretches from the Cape Cod Canal to Provincetown. It offers a different world to the sailor.

The cape juts out into the Atlantic in the familiar shape of an extended arm, bent at the elbow. What would correspond to the biceps and inner forearm—each representing about 30 miles of coastline—meet at right angles, enclosing two sides of Cape Cod Bay. The bay ranges from 30 to 150 feet deep, almost without shoal or obstruction. It is bordered on the western side above the canal by the

Plymouth shoreline, which extends 35 miles to Minot's Ledge at the beginning of Boston's harbor. The northern end of the bay leads to Massachusetts Bay and the Gulf of Maine.

A perfect place to sail at first look. It has no hazards like the shoals and islands which ring Nantucket Sound. Here is open, deep water, over nine hundred square miles of it, protected from ocean swells. Yet, in fact, far fewer sailboats are seen here than in Nantucket Sound or virtually any other North American body of water so suitably located.

This is all the more remarkable because many of the original Cape Cod seafaring men came from the inside shore. Starting in the 1790s, towns such as Dennis, Brewster, Barnstable, and Sandwich sent sea captains to Boston and New York in greater numbers than did any other section of the country. When the sailing ship era died in the late 1800s, Route 6A through these towns was well dotted with spacious captains' houses complete with widow's walks. Into them the great captains retired one by one to look out over the bay, live out their days, and often start new enterprises. The towns their riches helped build were picturesque, quiet, and tree-lined and are now antiquely beautiful.

When summer resort development came to the cape, it grew fastest not here but on the south shore, where land was less expensive, beaches as good, and the water just deep enough for recreational sailors in numerous harbors. By 1930 one found on the bay side only a few small sailboats at Provincetown and Wellfleet, a few at Dennis and Barnstable, a small fleet at a camp in Brewster. Not until crossing to the mainland at Plymouth, Duxbury, and Cohasset did one find significant numbers. Why was—why is—this pleasant bay so thinly populated by sailors?

Certainly not because of a lack of breezes. In summer the pressure-gradient winds rotating around the big high lingering near Bermuda, abetted by thermals drawn by the land masses of New England and the Canadian Maritime Provinces, create a strong southwester that blows easily over the low-lying cape. It drops to water level within a few yards of the bay shoreline, blowing at a merry clip. Only six-inch to one-foot waves are encountered as far as a half mile from the north-facing shore even in a spanking twenty-knot breeze. Sailing is ideal in the combined circumstance of strong breeze and smooth water. Strong onshore northerlies—rare in summer—make waves, but these are the only winds that do, and wave heights do not usually exceed three feet. Along the far inside shore at Provincetown or Wellfleet the opposite holds; the northerlies and easterlies produce flat water, the southwesterlies bring waves.

The problem with offshore breezes, as we have noted, is that inexperienced sailors can be lulled into going out too far. Whether this has actually happened often enough to frighten away small-boat sailors from Cape Cod Bay, I do not know. I suspect an instinctive caution is struck in almost every adult upon encountering this combination of conditions. But you cannot count on it, especially not in younger people. I know of two canoeists who, during the years I sailed at a camp along this coastline, went too far offshore. They could not paddle back against increasing waves and wind. They were teenagers, young women from another camp three miles up the shore. A rescue failed when their camp outboard was unable to sight the canoe, probably by then overturned in the choppy, white-capped water. When a Coast Guard Duck arrived some two hours later, it too could not find the canoe. It was found two days later on the Wellfleet shore, ten miles across the bay. The bodies of the young women were washed ashore several days after that on the banks of Namskaket Creek, four miles down the beach from their starting point. The camp closed within a week, never to reopen.

Recently two lives were lost in a similar way. According to a report in the *Cape Cod Times* on August 22, 1980, two people set out from the North Truro beach in a boardboat with the wind at twenty-five knots from the northeast—directly offshore from the Truro beach. The young man, twenty-three, and woman, twenty-one, were seen from the beach to tip over and recover twice. They capsized a third time, but no one could be seen climbing back aboard. A boat put out from the beach to rescue. Forty minutes later the boardboat was picked up by a fishing boat three miles offshore; that is how fast these boardboats will blow away from you in a high wind. No one was on or near the boat; one life jacket was found.

Sailing is inhibited along the bay's shore by tidal flats. Someone who has not seen the flats cannot guess at the size of the problem. At low tide the sandy plains extend nearly a mile offshore in some places. If your boat is moored along this shoreline, it may stand high and dry for half the day. Tides here rise and fall eight to twelve feet. The flats are caused by the extremely gradual incline of the bay's floor. Your bare feet are delightfully tickled by the little ridges left in the sand as the waves recede, and being able to walk to your boat is certainly convenient. But what do you do when you get there and find it sitting on a sea of sand?

One solution is to use inner and outer moorings. The outer is placed far enough out for the boat to be in a couple of feet of water even at low tide. The inner is placed at half the distance to shore. You must plan where to moor when coming in from a sail, depending on the predicted tide when you next intend to sail. If the tide crosses you up, your boat will either be hopelessly aground at the inner mooring, or perhaps a mile's dinghy ride away at the outer. This stimulates careful study of the tide tables. It also develops talent in planning ahead.

Despite these laudable disciplines, the flats have probably dampened small-boat activity along the inside shore more than any factor. Few harbors have channels that are usable at all tides for small boats, so few that they accommodate a relatively tiny boat population. Some harbors that had deep water in the nineteenth century have shoaled since. Only Provincetown now has a sizable "deep"-water boat harbor. Barnstable and Wellfleet have dredged channels into moderately sized boat basins, as have Sesuit and Rock Harbor on a smaller scale. Thus, in about sixty miles of coastline from Cape Cod Canal to Provincetown, there are only five harbors—not much to work with. No wonder we see fewer sailboats here than on the south shore, which has literally three times as many suitable harbors in a much shorter stretch.

The cape has a third and fourth side as well. The third lies along the Buzzards Bay shore on the back side of the cape's shoulder if you follow the bent-arm analogy. This coast is dotted with harbors from Woods Hole to the west end of the canal. They are filled with sailboats, contributing to the many seen on Buzzards Bay on almost any summer day. The harbors are small, indented between rocky fingers of land a little harsher than the sand-fringed boundaries of the cape's other coasts. They have names like Quisset, West Falmouth, Megansett, Pocasset, and Phinneys. Many Beetlecats, Bullseyes, Sunfish, and some small cruising boats are found here, as well as some avid sailors. They have to be avid, for they face the teeth-rattling Buzzards Bay chop any day when the wind blows southwest against an ebbing tide!

The fourth side is the Outer Beach, twenty miles of almost unbroken white sand from Nauset to Provincetown made famous in the writings of Wyman Richardson, Henry David Thoreau and Henry Beston. This is a land of crashing Atlantic surf, of high dunes and uplands precipitously hanging clifflike over the wide beach, of sand nearly too hot to walk on in summer, washed by water almost too cold to swim in. Not a single harbor is found along the Outer Beach from Chatham to Provincetown. The only break in the beach is at Nauset Inlet, which will take a knowledgeable boatman in a shallow draft skiff safely into the Orleans town cove. It is a shore for sailors to avoid, for all boatmen to shun. Exposed to prevailing easterly storms, without shelter, plagued by slanting onshore currents, pounded by waves that roll across a fetch from Europe's shore, this beach has claimed the bones of many a sailor and ship. In Beston's day, the nearest and only neighbor to the outermost house was a Coast Guard lifeboat station at Nauset. From there a nightly foot patrol was sent out along the beach in search of disaster and shipwreck. The Coast Guard station still stands, and the dangers have not changed. Just recently I heard the radio broadcast the news of recovery off Highland Light (a station further up the beach) of the leg bone of a fisherman lost last winter. His boat had failed to return to Provincetown. The bone, with a telltale fracture matching that of the missing man, was brought up from two-hundred-foot depths by another fishing boat's net. For one of these small, thirty- or forty-foot vessels to be fishing off the Outer Beach in the month of February is an act of courage, if not foolhardiness. The temporary mild spells can suddenly turn into fierce winter storms. On a hot July day, looking from atop the highlands towering over the Outer Beach at the small figures of sunbathers some three hundred feet below on the sand and gazing at the wondrously blue Atlantic stretching away to the horizon, one sees a scene of dazzling beauty. The tranquility of the moment belies the powerful forces now at rest. This shoreline is not for recreational sailors. The few who sail along it in summer must pick the day carefully. It is not a place to be caught when the storm winds blow.

Cape Cod Bay, however, someday may support more sailing activity. It awaits extensive harbor development along the inside shore from Sandwich to Provincetown or the solution of the inner-outer mooring dilemma. If that ever happens, the broad and protected bay waters should become a sailor's mecca. The bay would make an ideal site for racing, even for a class requiring fifteen- or twenty-mile course legs. A natural bowl, surrounded on three sides by land, largely unaffected by currents or ocean waves, full of breeze—what a grand amphitheater it would make for the America's Cup competition. By using particular course layouts, spectators on land could see the start, windward mark, and reaching mark.

Perhaps it will occur someday . . . no doubt with a cable-TV satellite hookup, a consortium of beer and gear sponsors, and the Dallas cowgirls to collect tickets at the bridges!

One Small Boat:
A Passage through Time

•

Our boat was built in the winter of 1913 and launched the following spring. Sixty-six years later, as I write, she is still actively sailed and raced. Lord knows how long, with proper care, a boat may go on.

How she came to her long life; who owned her; what adventures she took part in—these questions naturally have come to mind. Over the years friends and acquaintances have volunteered information. But the story remained tantalizingly incomplete for a long time. I resolved to trace the tale of this one small boat.

With the help of many people, not least Jamie Hess, who has traced the histories of my boat's entire class, the pieces finally fell into place. Hess's painstaking research in the early 1970s of the current lineage of every Senior built was published in 1976. It listed the then owner of each accurately numbered Senior. I am much indebted to him.

The Wianno Senior class has been successful. The Crosbys conceived and built them along the lines of the best gaff-rigged racing boats of the time, and they have outlasted many. Our own boat is far from alone in her antiquity. Of the 14 boats built the first winter 8 still sail. Of the 160 built between 1914 and 1976, only 15 are known wrecked, lost, burned, or abandoned. Most of the remaining 145 boats are still sailing. About 55 boats race regularly, including 2 launched in 1914. One built in 1930, Dave Steere's *Venture* (85), was grandly sailed to victory in the last tough race of the 1979 regatta season by her owner, who is quite possibly more than a decade older than his boat.

This remarkable longevity in years and numbers testifies to the integrity in design and construction of the boats. And, obviously, their owners have loved and cared for them well. One Senior—the late Jim Hinkle's *Fantasy* (11)—is now on exhibit at the Mystic Seaport Museum, part of a display of notable small sailing craft. Another— John F. Kennedy's blue-hulled *Victura* (94), beautifully rebuilt and refinished—points seaward on her tilted pedestal on the grass in front of the Kennedy Library at the edge of Boston harbor, a haunting, lone, riderless steed stopped in full stride.

Other good classes from the early times have also survived—the Herreshoff S-boats and Bullseyes; the Stars; the big Idem gaffers of 1898 in upper New York—but none more impressively than the Seniors with regard to the proportion of the original boats still sailing over a like span of years. So the fact that ours, number 7, survives is not so much remarkable as it is typical and illustrative.

The boat's first owner was apparently Jack Tiernan of

Osterville, Massachusetts, and Cairo, Illinois. I must say *apparently* because the first written record I have found connecting Jack Tiernan to the boat's ownership goes back to 1915 rather than 1914. This leaves the possibility that someone else owned her during the first year. The late, beloved Max Crosby, who helped to build all the first boats while in his teens and whose fairness and skill played a vital part in the construction of nearly every Senior thereafter, told me in the mid-1970s that he thought there might have been an owner before Jack Tiernan. But the name always escaped Uncle Max, and there seems to be no one else to remember. It was a long time ago.

The cost of a new Senior in 1914 was $650. A letter from Jack Tiernan's cousin and sometime crew gives a little of the history and flavor of those times:

Mount Dora, Florida
April 29th, 1974

Dear Mr. Ulian—

I do thank you for your very interesting letter concerning the history of #7 Crosby cat. As Ann has probably told you our family travelled from Cairo, Illinois to Osterville, first by train, then by car. We spent our first years at East Bay Lodge and my memory recalls 1915. I was 13 years old. My cousin John Craig Aisthorpe was 11—we were then crew in #7 operated by Cousin Jack Tiernan.

My last summer with Cousin Jack was the summer of 1924. 1925 I spent in Europe. We returned to the Cape in 1926. Father rented Ralph Crosby's house. 1927 and 1928 I visited with Ann's grandmother in her house on East Bay and still remember #7 and Cousin Jack.

Then 1929 with two friends we stayed at the Crosby House for golf and I do not remember sailing with Cousin Jack nor with Ann.

Then the stock break and I was in the brokerage business in Chicago. So I did not see the Cape again until 1935.

Those were wonderful years and wish my memory was more complete and exact.

[Signed]
Russell Halliday

The *Ann* mentioned in the letter is Anne Pillow Halliday, a friend, a Wianno summer resident in the early 1900s, a vigorous year-round resident now. With her help I contacted Russell Halliday, who in turn provided some of the first clues to the boat's early history.

Jack Tiernan named his boat *Patsy*. The notebooks of the Wianno Yacht Club list *Patsy* in the racing results for the years 1917-1922 under her original sail number, 7, skippered by "J. Tiernan." From 1923-1929, the notebooks list her still as *Patsy*, now carrying sail number 29, "J. Tiernan, skipper." In those years, when you bought a new sail, you got a new number with it.

Jack Tiernan had fallen in love as a boy with the beauty of the Great Lakes schooners of the day. According to Anne Halliday, he kept *Patsy* neat and pretty, even flaking down lines with a precision good schooner crews might have envied. He took pleasure in his boat, sailing often, fussing over it much. I am glad of that, because he did not do too well at the races according to the notebooks, not even after buying his new sail!

In 1929 or 1930, whether because of the market crash or for other reasons, Jack Tiernan sold his boat to the Morris Ernst family of Nantucket and New York City. By the time I called Mr. Ernst in the spring of 1974, the lawyer had forgotten the details of the family's ownership of *Patsy*. But he was interested in the boat's history. "You ought to write a biography of the boat for one of the sailing magazines," he said. Then he asked me to write him a brief letter relating "just the facts found so far." I promised to do my best. In May, 1976, I finally did write him the facts I had discovered. Mr. Ernst's secretary replied. He had died that spring.

Later, Morris Ernst's son Roger very kindly furnished some of his memories of the boat. Roger Ernst must have been very young at the time, but he recalled *Patsy* fondly. The family kept her moored in Nantucket harbor in front of their house and sailed in her often and with pleasure. He has graciously asked us to sail over and revisit her old home, which we hope to do someday.

Roger Ernst could not recall exactly when the family sold *Patsy*. But her next owners did. Young Carl Barus, of Bass River and Upper Montclair, New Jersey, bought her in 1938 with most of his life's savings. Mrs. Jane Barus, his mother, and one of the great ladies of New Jersey, tells the story of how it happened and how *Patsy*'s name came to be changed:

> Upper Montclair, N. J.
> September 11, 1975

Dear Dick—

I promised to write you the story about the original name of Carl's boat—so here it is. When he was a baby we started a little savings account for him, and by the summer of 1938 it amounted to (I believe) $800.00. By this time he had followed the family tradition and had become an excellent sailor—having been coached by his fa-

ther, who was also very good at the helm. So he
bought the Senior Wianno then named *Patsy*. I
believe it took all of his savings account. He had
that spring taken what was known as the
Johnson-O'Connor aptitude tests at Stevens In-
stitute and had found (to his own surprise I think)
that he had a good musical ear and memory. The
opera *Die Valkyrie* appealed to him at the
time—and so the brass *Patsy* letters were removed and the boat was named *Valkyrie*. Carl
practically lived on her in the summers—and
took many long cruises. But my husband, who
was a hoarder of everything that could
possibly—however improbably—come in useful, kept the old letters. Carl graduated from
Brown and enlisted in the Navy, and we took
over the boat for him. He was in the Pacific for
four years, and then became a radar instructor
for naval officers in this country until after the
war was over. From that time on he did not have
the leisure to care for the boat himself. And at
some point—I can't remember just when—his
father and I decided we had had enough of
racing—having been at it since our teens—and
we sold the *Valkyrie*, as you know, and bought a
Junior Wianno—which was the only one on the
river—and hence couldn't be raced. As I remember it, she had no name at the time and there
was much family discussion about what to call
her. We had formerly had a Cape Cod knocka-
bout called *Sea Pup*, so we thought of *Sea Dog*
etc. etc. But Peter Barus—Carl's second son—
came up with SALTY! This *delighted* his grand-

father, who forthwith produced the PATSY letters. So we used the S, A, T, and Y—and bought a brass L! No doubt the P is still lurking around somewhere.

Incidentally, 1938 was the year of the first hurricane to hit the Cape in 100 years. Carl and I took the *Valkyrie* out and proved that you can lay a Wianno down flat and bring her up again. It was quite a sail.

Sorry this is such a messy scrawl. I'm getting to be a shaky old crone—and my hand isn't steady.

The best of luck to you and the Wianno #7.—

Sincerely—
Jane Barus

P.S. Correction—
Carl says the boat cost only $650. He bought her the summer before his Sophomore year at Brown.

The Barus family sailed the boat until 1953. The years saw a cruise to Maine undertaken by Carl Barus with two friends, and many races at Bass River in which *Valkyrie* was successful against others of her class, apparently with Carl's skillful father Max often at her tiller. The boat was moored in the river opposite the Barus compound along the west bank. She has in recent years gone back to lie at their dock during the biannual Bass River regatta. Some of the present members of the Barus family still enjoy going for a sail on her at regatta time and are very welcome too.

On August 5, 1963, *Valkyrie* was sold to Robert L. Small of West Dennis, Massachusetts:

August 5, 1953

In consideration of the sum of Five Hundred Dollars ($500.00) and the payment by the purchaser of one half of the broker's $50.00 commission, receipt whereof is hereby acknowledged, I hereby sell my Wianno Senior Knock-about, "Valkyrie", together with her sails, equipment, and mooring, to Robert L. Small, of West Dennis, Cape Cod, Massachusetts, all as now located at Ship Shops Inc., Bass River, Cape Cod, Massachusetts, together with any and all her sails, if any, that may be elsewhere in my possession. I certify that the boat is free and clear of all debts and other encumbrances, and that her storage is paid up in full to date of sale. I am making no other warranties as to the condition of the property sold.

Maxwell Barus

Bob Small is the son of the late Joe Small, a well-known Cape Cod sailor of the day who had been commodore of the Bass River Yacht Club and a president of the Southern Massachusetts Yacht Racing Association. The Commodore Joseph E. Small Memorial Trophy, competed for by southern Massachusetts sailors, is today the single-handed championship trophy of the district.

Bob Small now lives in Huntington, Long Island. He has told me that, when he put the boat in the water, she had been laid up for three years. She had big spaces between all her planks, as much as one-inch spaces between her keel boards. Her paint was hanging like moss. She sunk for one month after being put in, then pulled together beautifully. Next year he had her refastened, and she was tight. She went fast, Bob Small recalls, particularly upwind, pointing exceptionally well. She won a number of trophies. But she was slow downwind—they lost several races that way. While he owned the Senior, Bob Small helped originate the present Bass River regatta.

The mast was in awful shape, rotted and weak, Bob recalls. It snapped one breezy day off Bass River when the boat hit a wave and stopped dead, but the mast kept going. Bob Small got her a new mast and new sails, using the number 7. He had her wooded down inside and out and added a cove stripe, gold-leafed. She looked beautiful.

In 1957 at Edgartown the boat had a serious accident. At the regatta, a thirty-footer came up under 7, which was on starboard tack, and plowed into the boat's middle, breaking the oak coaming, toe rail, boom, and sail track, and twisting the centerboard. A girl was thrown out of the boat on impact. Joe Small was at 7's tiller, and son Bob was worried for his safety because the larger boat came right back aboard after the first impact. The Senior righted itself, however, and the other boat rode up so high it went directly above Commodore Small's head without touching him. No one was hurt. The repair bill was $421, Bob remembers, and the boat did not leak afterwards.

When he started work on his Ph.D., Bob Small found he had sailed the Senior only three times in two summers. So on October 3, 1959, he sold her to Arthur W. Frostholm for $1550.

The Frostholm family lived in West Yarmouth year-round. Arthur Frostholm recalls that he sailed the boat for one season, the summer of 1959, during which the family had fun with it. The following winter she stayed outside in his backyard—probably her first winter outdoors in thirty-six years. Her next owners, James P. Ryan and his wife Peg, bought her from Frostholm on February 19, 1961.

Peg Ryan remembers the date well, because on that

evening the Ryans celebrated their engagement with dinner at Eugene's, a restaurant in Middleboro halfway between Boston and Cape Cod. Given its double signifi-cance, the dinner was a great success. On April 17, 1961, the Ryans sailed 7 from Cape Cod to Continental Marina, Quincy, near their home in Jamaica Plain, outside of Bos-ton. She was solid and tight; no trace of a leak. They sailed her all that summer and the next in Quincy Bay and Boston harbor. But in 1963, when they launched her, she would not stop leaking.

First Jim Ryan, who had done his own maintenance work, and then the people at Continental Marina tried to stop the leaking, which was caused by rot around the centerboard box. Nothing worked. The boat would not float. The Ryans by now were in love with their Senior. They had just bought a pretty green and white spinnaker. On St. Patrick's Day, 1963, or soon after, they looked forward to cutting a fine figure sailing in the harbor. Not yet prepared to give up their dream, they loaded the boat on a flatbed trailer and at some expense had her brought to Crosbys yard for repair.

Theirs had been a long engagement. Three weeks before the wedding date, the Crosbys informed Jim Ryan of the probable cost of repairs. It left him with a difficult decision concerning the allocation of his resources. Jim Ryan's wife says he still jokes that he made the wrong choice the day he traded the Senior to Doug Higham, a boat carpenter at Crosbys. He got in return a sound little Bigelow catboat, which Peg remembers as eighteen feet long and cute, and he conserved enough money to launch their marriage successfully. They still keep the green and white spinnaker in the basement. It has never been out of its bag.

Doug Higham was—and is—an experienced boat-

builder. He put the Senior in the yard at his house in
Osterville and went to work. With the help and advice of
his two sons, Bill Crosby, and other friends and boatyard
workers who dropped by from time to time, he performed
a major rebuild and a minor miracle. The keel was removed, as were the garboards, the sheer planks, the cockpit sole and bulkheads, and the entire deck and cuddy
cabin. Then all these parts were built again new using the
original patterns.

The centerboard box was thought to be too far gone
to replace or rebuild without opening up the possibility of
future loss of the boat. Higham therefore removed the box
and plugged up the opening in the keelson. He built a new
centerboard to fit the remaining slot in the keel and dead-
wood. It had the same doweled oak construction and
length as a normal Senior board but only about half the
lateral plane. This is what Jamie Hess has called a half-
centerboard. Number 7 is the only boat in the fleet so
rebuilt, although at least thirteen of the older ones now
have no centerboards at all, their keelson slots having been
plugged.

Higham felt pleased with his work, having with one
stroke eliminated the large box, which took up so much
room inside the cuddy and the cockpit and is always
subject to leaking, and made the boat tight again.

In the spring of 1964 she was launched, freshly
painted, gleaming white. As a cruising sailor who almost
never raced, Higham rigged her to cruise, paying no mind
to racing gear or tune. In fact, in his opinion the boat would
not be competitive. He particularly anticipated a problem
in staying with the fleet upwind with the new
half-centerboard.

Over the years we have brought her up, little by little,
to something nearer racing tune. As for winning, she has

recently won some junior-skipper races against other good Seniors with Steve at the tiller. In time, as he and his crews gain more experience, she might again give a creditable account of herself against the adult skippers.

In July of 1964 I first saw 7 at Crosbys and sailed her. I determined to buy her then. I have related how I finally succeeded in doing so. But not before Giles Wanamaker, formerly of Greenwich and just moved to Orleans, saw her sitting prettily at Crosbys with the name *Valkyrie* on her transom. The very same name as that of his former yacht, which he had just sold in Greenwich! He inquired how much. Doug Higham figured he was entitled to X number of dollars per hour for his labors; he estimated a thousand hours had been worked, and he did his multiplication. Giles Wanamaker promptly wrote a check for the product.

Either that fall or in the spring of 1965, Wanamaker and Higham sailed 7 eastward to Stage Harbor, Chatham. They walked her through the channel behind Morris Island and sailed up Pleasant Bay. She was moored in the small pond where I found her three years later.

Giles Wanamaker lavished attention on the boat. The cove stripe of Bob Small's day was again leafed with gold. A gold-leafed quarterboard went on her transom, the carving done by Doug Higham. Many coats of varnish were carefully laid on her brightwork by a Norwegian working for the Arey's Pond boatyard. He had a special touch with a brush. Every aspect of her care was lovingly done.

In late June, 1967, I purchased the boat from Giles Wanamaker. I received the following brief document:

Orleans, Mass.
June 30, 1967
Received from Richard Ulian the sum of
one dollar and other valuable considerations, in

payment in full for one Wianno Senior, hull number 7, named "Valkyrie."

[Signed]
Giles A. Wanamaker

I sailed her back to Osterville, arriving on July 4, 1967. She has sailed from Osterville the past fourteen summers, attended to and maintained by one or the other Crosby yards and increasingly, by Steve and myself. She remained perfectly tight for ten or eleven years. She has started to weep at the garboards rather more than we like now, but she is getting attention, and we hope a bit of caulking will solve the problem.

Although she has raced semiregularly with the rest of the fleet for most of the years in Osterville, she is a family boat, not strictly a racing vehicle. We use her for pleasure sailing, for giving lessons, for whatever comes along, and like all the Seniors, she responds handsomely.

Her name is new. When I first saw *Valkyrie* on her transom, I was not as entranced as Giles Wanamaker. Collector of slain heroes was not the role I had in mind for the boat, Valhalla not my first choice of cruising destinations.

I resolved to change it, though three years before Doug Higham had asked me not to, recounting the boatman's tale of bad luck accompanying a name change. I believe he thought *Valkyrie* was her original name. None of us knew then about *Patsy*. I checked with the men at Crosbys. Put any name you want on it, they said; just do it while she is on dry land and you will not have any bad luck.

During that summer I searched the Osterville Library for a suitable name. There I found the story of a certain Miss Lovell of the village. In 1818, it seems, she married Andrew Crosby, one of the early members of the boat-building family. Late in life, the story goes, Andrew Crosby drew the plans for a new kind of Crosby boat. Shortly thereafter, he and his wife joined the Spiritualism movement, popular at the time. The members believed the living could communicate with the spirits of the dead. Mrs. Crosby became a medium, able, it was said, to establish this connection. Andrew died before his new boat could be built. His two sons, Horace and Worthington, went to work to build the boat and thus prove the design's ability. When they encountered an insoluble problem in the construction, legend says Mrs. Crosby held a seance in order to receive instructions from Andrew.

The boat was launched in 1850, and it was a great success. She sailed faster than the previous boats "thrice for one," we are told, and came about "quick as a cat," giving origin to the naming of the many boats the Crosbys built subsequently that followed her design: cat boats. It marked a turning point in their business.

In the prevailing biblical fashion of those Cape Cod days, Mrs. Andrew Crosby's given name was Tirzah. During the spring of 1968, while number 7 was most assuredly on dry land, Teddy Crosby, Tirzah's great-great-grandson, I believe, carved the letters *T I R Z A* on our boat's transom. They were then gold-leafed. Number 7 had her new name.

It doubly pleased me. In the late 1940s and the 1950s during the War of Independence in that part of the world I had made several trips to Israel. A revival of biblical Hebrew had occurred there. I recalled in particular a young woman named Tirza. (The current Israeli-English spelling of the name drops the *h*.) She was one of the most capable leaders of a small kibbutz at the foot of Mount Tabor, where I lived for some time and was shown great hospitality. I admired her determination and good sense and was happy that she and Mrs. Crosby shared the boat's name.

Later, when we discovered her original name was *Patsy*, it seemed too late to change *Tirza* back. The kids would not hear of it. Now, if the people at the Crosby yards would pronounce it *Teer-tsa*, the old way, instead of *Ter-za*, which seems to have come down from Cape Cod of the 1850s, I would be completely happy. It means delight.

The Cruise of the *Argo*

·

Suppose you are an experienced small-boat sailor. You would like to try sailing a large cruising boat, but you do not know if you can handle it. Nonetheless, on the strength of your experience in little boats, your friends charter a forty-eight footer from a much too trusting acquaintance of theirs. Autumn has come to New England, a time of tranquil spells broken by sudden storms.

I once sailed a cruising boat under those circumstances. With one exception, my friends and crew were inexperienced. The scenes that I recall go something like this.

Marblehead. The puddles in the parking area reflect a gray, drizzly September sky. A northeast wind ominously curls fog fingers around the streetlights. Through the murky dusk I see the crew's car. I lift the duffle out of my own car and start down the ramp. We're here, all right. But can we sail the boat that lies along the dock at the ramp's end?

Argo Navis is a wood ketch, twenty-five tons of boat. My experience is mostly in boats of up to sixteen feet weighing about five hundred pounds. I have sailed thirty footers and a thirty-six footer on widely separated occasions. My crew's limited experience is also in small sailboats. George has done Navy time on shore launches and other powerboats. The rest of the group's sailing time totals a few outings in Lightning-class boats: Ben and his wife Hilary have done some of this sailing; George's wife Dede, a little; Sandy and Carol are starting fresh from the dock.

The weather on this foggy first night certainly looks forbidding. I feel anxious. Then I see George and Ben, blurred shadows on the deck. Their welcome is almost enough to calm me.

George has already done the boat checkout with the owner, who has left nonchalantly for a cocktail party. I am glad he is casual; still, I do not know whether to be relieved or more worried.

"He said we might have trouble with the throttle," George says. "The linkage broke. They wired it temporarily a couple of weeks ago."

Ugh.

"No other problems we know of," George said. "The tanks are topped off. I've been over the boat and I think I know where everything is. There won't be any activity at the town dock tonight, the owner says. He thinks we can lie here overnight."

I look the boat over. The *Argo* had been strongly built

for a circumnavigation thirty years ago. She made it as far as the Galapagos. She had been bought and sold a few times since then and she looks husky but a little tired.

My knowledge of larger cruising boats comes chiefly from a few swift readings of the applicable chapters in H. A. Calahan's *Learning to Sail.* Everything on deck seems to be as Calahan predicted. Other than the boom-gallows and varnished wheel, the gear is familiar to a small-boat sailor but oversize. After a few minutes I start to feel better.

"Want to go below?" Ben asks. "We've got the radio tuned in to the weather. Well, how do you like her?"

"Looks okay. Big, isn't she?"

Ben made a reassuring face. He was the one who got the boat for us through a business connection. His faith in my sailing ability had no known limits. He led the way below.

While Hilary served up coffee and doughnuts, the radio broadcast good cheer. A fair and warm day was forecast for tomorrow.

We were cozy and dry in the cabin. Soon we made up the bunks and turned in to sleep.

The boat lay bow towards shore, but the stern extended several feet beyond the dock's outer end. We could not then pull ahead. At low tide there was insufficient water under the bow. Naturally, at three in the morning, when the tide was high, a lobsterman thumped on our hull. We sleepily pushed the boat forward so the dock would be clear for his boat to come in and load traps. He groused quite rightly that we should not tie up at the town dock overnight.

Morning dawned calm and sunny. Sandy and Carol now joined us. After breakfast we cast off and slowly backed out.

Very slowly. Calahan's advice is to proceed as in a small boat—but much more slowly. Very sound advice.

I was surprised at how easily *Argo* handled. Her great bulk glided gently from the dock. The wind was light, which helped my confidence. Under power, we inched carefully around the moored boats still crowded in the harbor. Soon we rounded Marblehead Neck. The sun came out. Lobster pot buoys dotted the sparkling channel. Peel sweaters, don bikinis.

We hoisted sails without trouble. We shut off the engine, and under main, mizzen, and big genny *Argo* heeled to a gentle northeast breeze, Provincetown bound. This was the life!

The big ketch seemed to move too sluggishly, however. Inspection revealed a line dragging from under the transom at an angle that suggested we were pulling something heavy. We hauled the line in, surprisingly hard to do, and found a lobster pot at its end. The line had snagged on our prop, no doubt. We cut it free, not wishing to poach from a lobsterman presumably ready to make his time-honored reply with a well-aimed shotgun.

We could not hazard starting the engine until the prop was cleared. It seemed unwise to send someone over the side a mile offshore in icy waters. Marblehead—narrow and full of boats—did not invite an attempt to reenter under sail alone. So we left the prop fouled and rolled lazily along, making the fifty or so miles to Race Point in one long tack. It was a lovely day for a first sail. By 4:00 we could see the spire of Provincetown Monument, a matchstick on the horizon. We had seen one boat all day, a commercial trawler.

It took two hours in the dying evening breeze to reach Wood End and then round Long Point, sheets eased, and head into the harbor. It was blessedly empty. We dropped the genny on the way in. Where the chart showed eight to ten feet depths off Provincetown Wharf, the helm went over and *Argo* docilely rounded up in the evening stillness. When she stopped, the anchor was let go and set. No problems from the lack of an engine yet.

We dinghied ashore for dinner. A somnolent postseason Provincetown echoed our footsteps up and down Commercial Street. We returned to the boat early and turned in.

The morning weather forecast called for a partly cloudy day with light northeast winds. But it also stated that small craft warnings might go up after noontime, with heavy squalls possible.

Our first priority was to clear the prop. No one wanted to get into the 50° water. At that temperature water will fast turn you blue with cold. George created a diversionary nuisance by raising the Race Point Coast Guard station on the radio and asking for a better suggestion. In short order a launch with six or seven Guardsmen appeared. Whether magnetized by our female contingent or simply happy to escape routine for a while, they lay off our port quarter and chatted for half an hour. Their advice, of course, was to jump in and clear the wrapped line. Or haul the boat. The latter idea seemed to tickle them greatly.

Sandy apparently was the one who had the wheel when the trap was snagged, so he volunteered. In three dives he cut and cleared the line away. He reported the water felt very, very cold.

A window-shopping trip among the half-closed sandal shops quickly exhausted Provincetown's lonely September charms. Our crew wanted to shove off. Boredom was setting in. The sky looked leaden. I felt that we might have a rough trip to Cape Cod Canal but agreed to try it if the majority wished. We voted to go.

As the *Argo* motored out, sunlight broke through the morning haze. Sails and bikinis were soon the order of the day. The air was cool, the sun warm. The wind was so light that, running dead before it, the boat scarcely moved, so we reached off toward Billingsgate Island, making slow progress.

By noon we had Wellfleet abeam. We jibed directly for the canal, bringing the breeze over the starboard quarter. Carol, the least experienced, took the helm. Everyone settled in for a pleasant afternoon's sail. None of us looked at a dark line of clouds over the Truro Highlands. I picked a sunny spot on deck and dozed.

The squall sneaked up silently. The first sound I remember was not the wind but the worried murmur of voices in the cockpit. I felt the heel of the boat increase. When I went back to the cockpit, George was already there.

"What do you think?" he asked.

"I'd like the genoa off, okay?"

"Ben and I will go forward and do it."

The wind came up very quickly to about thirty knots. The Wellfleet shore disappeared behind us in the scud. Visibility forward closed down to about a quarter mile. Ahead lay twenty miles of unbuoyed, although unobstructed, water before we would reach the canal entrance. It lay on a lee shore. An interesting variety of short, steep seas was making up astern.

The size of the boat now began to bother me. I could not see Ben and George out on the bowsprit; a vast and cluttered distance lay between us. Sandy positioned himself amidship to relay messages, but his shouts were not audible against the rush of wind and the slap of luffing sails.

The bow plunged deeply under oncoming seas and the security of the men on the bowsprit seemed threatened. They wore no safety harnesses, which were largely unknown then. I throttled back to ease the motion of the boat, and the temporary repair on the throttle linkage promptly let go. We continued to power ahead too fast. Later I heard that the bowsprit went deep under twice. But the genny was finally secured, and then with Sandy's help the mainsail was wrestled to the boom and safely furled.

Under motor and mizzen we ran before the storm. *Argo*'s heavily built, slab-sided hull produced a markedly erratic motion. The extra push imparted by the engine only added to the problem, but I did not want to cut it for fear it might not start again when required in the canal. Nor did I feel I could leave it in neutral; the throttle was set too high.

If there was one direction this vessel seemed to want to go, it was down. Something in the way she fought the wheel and yawed headstrong, headlong down the following seas gave me that sinking feeling. Whether this was an accurate judgment or merely the offshoot of my anxiety, I do not know. I wonder where *Argo* is now, and how she has weathered her subsequent storms.

The wind leveled off at about forty knots. I was busily spinning spokes when I felt the gaze of a pale-faced Dede fixed on me. She was standing braced in the companionway, her expression posing a question that appeared to be, Are we going to survive? I peered off into the blank fog with all the confidence I could summon. It seemed to satisfy her. With feigned nonchalance I reached up and touched the mizzen over my head with one hand. The sail was stiff as a board under the intensity of the wind's pressure. I jerked my hand away as if I had touched a hot frying pan.

Below, Ben moved the engine cover and crawled into a narrow space in an attempt to fix the throttle linkage. After a half hour he came up looking slightly seasick. Next day in calm water he was able to take care of the repair in ten minutes.

After two hours on a roughly averaged compass course we were drawing close to the canal entrance between Sandwich and Sagamore. We peered into the white wooly mist and listened for the sound of breakers on the beach. After perhaps twenty minutes of strain we saw apparitionlike in midair—two hundred feet above the fog-hidden shoreline—a ghostly gray outline of the steel super-structure that carries Sagamore Bridge across the canal. A moment later shore was in sight. The canal entrance buoy was one hundred yards ahead.

This practically ended our cruise. We lay at Onset for the next two days waiting for the weather to abate. It did not. Our charter was for a long four-day weekend only, so I called the owner. He gave his okay to leave *Argo* tied up at the boatyard there, saying he had plans to cruise in that area later in the season.

The next summer I chartered a fifty-four-foot Alden schooner. We cruised Buzzards Bay and Nantucket Sound, greatly enjoying the vessel and the weather. Within a couple of days the boat's size no longer seemed awesome.

But it seems wiser not to leap into fifty-footers without first sailing the intermediate sizes, which are readily available from the charter companies. Later in the evening on which the *Argo* sailed wearily into Onset at the far end of the canal, a boyhood friend of mine—a lieutenant commander in the naval reserve—who was in command of a sizable patrol boat on training exercises off Marblehead, had the misfortune to have his vessel go on the rocks and sink. No lives were lost, but his commission was—after a court martial. His experience was overmatched by the size of the vessel under his command in that kind of weather off a rocky coast. The same thing could have happened to me or to anyone out on that miserable night. Without the experience to handle his vessel in tough conditions or in a vessel not capable of meeting the conditions, a sailor is risking his life, his crew's, and those of his possible rescuers.

Since the cruise of the *Argo* I have made some effort not to let that combination of circumstances occur again on a boat that I sail. I hope what has been related here will persuade you to do likewise.

·23·

Companionship and Sailing

•

Sailing is not necessarily companionable, at least not in the usual sense of conversational chitchat. One of the chief pleasures of an afternoon's sail is its quietness. The lapping waves, a creaking block, sails luffing during a tack—these are the sounds of a happy boat. Small talk comes best when you are back on land, drinking beer, comparing notes at a party or bar.

The sounds of sailing also tell a story of the boat's speed, orientation to wind and wave, and general well-being. That is one reason to listen attentively. But only one. Pure pleasure in the absence of life's usual clatter is the other.

You will notice further proof of this if, having powered out the channel in an auxiliary with several friends, you cut the engine and set sail. The ensuing silence brings expressions of relief from everyone. Sail on a while. Watch your friends each find a quiet spot on deck. One will stand at the bow rail and gaze at the ocean. Another will take the windward rail; one may perhaps prefer the leeward. Even those remaining in the cockpit are generally laconic as they fold into the sensation of motion under sail.

Occasionally you go sailing with someone who cannot stop talking or one whose company stimulates lots of conversation. You both return to shore frustrated, having missed something important. You are perhaps not the best-matched sailing companions.

Yet sailing provides much companionship. You share the feeling of being at one with the forces of nature. The soft embrace of water hugging a good hull, the thoroughbred action of the hull itself, is transmitted and received from person to person. Oral comments may be few, but as the vessel heels to the wind you are all borne not just on the same boat but on a common tide of feeling. Sometimes—as the boat leans, breeze freshens, waves slap—this swells until it seems the emotion alone could transport you transatlantic. There are whoops and shouts of pleasure, smiles to pass along.

This is the best companionship of sail, the community of a lively vessel and its crew, waterborne.

Finish Line

•

Last autumn a man wanting to learn to sail called me. He had just bought a daysailer and moored it in East Bay up toward the Centerville River. Would I come down and teach him even though the season had grown late?

September Sundays were warm last fall. After the morning Beetle races I took the Whaler out the cut and turned east, running down a mile or so of the Wianno shore past some houses grand and old, past Dowses Beach, into the East Bay cut. On the beach at the landing I espied a slim, wiry, intense, and slightly nervous man in his early fifties. His companion was younger, mustachioed, relaxed.

On the daysailer it became apparent that the older man had read the sailing instruction books and become overcautious. In contrast, his son-in-law was as calm, understanding, and open—and laid back about sailing—as ever a first-time sailor could be. He took the tiller first.

The breeze had come up, so we sailed in the bay and up the river. Easy going for son-in-law, father's worries evaporating. Now father on the tiller. A few bloops, and then steady progress beating up the river, running back down, reaching across the bay. Finally they brought the boat in, moored, and furled by themselves.

I did not get a call for the next two weeks, and I thought my student had decided to sail on his own. But then came another call. This time father was alone and once again worried.

But the wind was light, the sailing easy. Soon it became clear that he could handle the boat alone quite well. I settled in as a passenger. He did it all, mooring, furling, putting the boat to bed.

In the remaining few weeks of decent weather I saw him weekends, puttering and fixing on his boat in the bay, occasionally sailing, looking unhurried and relaxed. His was the very last sailboat in East Bay to be taken in off its mooring for the winter. I think he has found his relaxation from onshore pressures. This spring I expect his boat to appear early on its mooring.

Earlier in the summer my son Mark came down with a friend for a couple of days on the cape. We piled in the Whaler to go out to meet Steve, coming in from a junior series race in number 7. It was blowing eighteen knots or so. Steve had won a race—the first one ever for any of us in 7. At the mooring, Mark and his friend jumped on, the racing crew debarked. Steve stayed and we all headed back down the channel for a sail. Mark had the tiller now after years away from it, the wind up to twenty, the boat on her ear, everybody all grins, even Mark's friend—on her first sail—happily awash on the leeward cockpit seat and refusing to move to the high dry side. A glorious sail! And to watch your kids enjoying it so!

One moonlit night after dinner, I slip down to the boat for a night sail. The silver path of moonbeams on West Bay points right out the cut. It is August, and already a coolness permeates the light night breeze.

Not many more opportunities will come along this season. I raise the main only and follow the silver-rippled path southwestward out the cut. All is silence but for the lapping wavelets against the hull; all blackness but for the silver glints on the water, the shadowy white of the sail, the starlight shining through pinholes pricked in the black, felt-domed universe. I sit quietly as the boat floats through space. We reach Bell One, shaking my reverie. The younger kids need putting to bed, someone in the house to secure them against the night. Besides, it is getting chilly out here, and lonely too.

I sail back to the mooring and put the boat to bed. From the Whaler, on the way in to the dock, I look back at her, so beautiful in repose.

Good night, boat. You have given much pleasure. Sleep quietly. We shall sail again in the morning.

$Index$

Aground, 108, 109
Airplane wing, as model of sail's
    forces, 88–89
Allen's Harbor, 22, 23
America, 67
America's Cup, 67
Anchor flukes, 30
Anchoring, 13, 28–31
Anchor line, 29, 44
Apparent wind, 94
Arey's Pond, 22, 57, 128
Argo Navis, 133–140 passim
Audobon Society, 80

Backstay pull, 51
Barnstable, 111, 112
Barus family, 121–124
Battens, 48
Bay of Fundy, 103, 106
Beam, 9

Beating, 10
Beetlecat, as learning boat, 18; as
    weekend racer, 71; at moorings,
    77; in Buzzards Bay, 114; in yacht
    club classes, 48, 50
Bermuda 40, 78, 112
Beston, Henry, 115
Block, for main sheet, 49
Boardboats, dangers of, 19, 45;
    popularity of, 19
Boom, danger in a jibe, 12; extra-
    long, 33, 55; mainsail furled on,
    138.
Boston, 102, 111, 126
Bow, 7
Bow wave, 15
Brewster, 56
Bulkhead, 48
Bullseye, 114, 118
Buzzards Bay, 114, 115, 139
Byrnes, Dan, 72

Index

Calahan, H.A., 134, 135
Camp Canduit, 82
Camp Havdunit, 82
Captain Kidd, 82
Caribbean islands, 103, 106
Carter, Dick, 18, 72
Cape Cod Bay, 110–116
Cape Cod Canal, 114, 137, 139
Centerville River, 143
Charts, 24, 25
Chatham, 22, 115, 128
Chee Chee IV, 73
Chichester, Sir Francis, 17
China Sea, 106
Chinese box kite, 89, 96
Coaming, 50, 61
Coast Guard, 17, 82, 112, 115, 136
Cockpit, 7, 15, 56
Cohasset, 111
Collier's Ledge, 151
Come about, 6
Compass, 24
Cotuit, 80; Bay, 80–82; cut, 81, 82; village, 82
Coulson, Bob, 72
Cowes, 67
Crosbys, 54, 82, 84, 85, 118–131; Andrew, 128; Bill, 54, 55, 127; Horace, 128; Joe's oyster house, 85; Max, 119; Teddy, 130; tug, 48; workboat, 55; Worthington, 128
Cuddy, 15, 56, 57; bench, 49

Dead Neck, 80, 81, 83
Delahanty, Captain, 4–6
Dennis, 111
Depth sounder, 24
Docking, 31–34
Downhaul, 87
Dowses Beach, 143
Duxbury, 111
Duxbury Duck, 56

East Bay, 143, 144
East Chop, 51
Ebb tide, 25
Edgartown, 31, 47, 51, 125; Regatta, 72, 125
Eel River, 77, 78
Ernst family, 120, 121

Falmouth, 54
Fantasy (11), 118
Fastnet Rock, 2, 72
Fend off, 32
Float, 32, 33
Flood tide, 25
Flotation, 41
Freeboard, 42, 48
Fog, 25–27
Frostholm, Arthur, 125

Gaff, mainsail, 33, 48, 50; peak, 49; sloop, 32
Galapagos (islands), 134
Garrison's Point, 50, 77, 79
Grand Island, 79, 80
Great Neck, 52
Gunwale, 49

Halliday family, 120
Halyards, 7
Hannah Screechum Island, 82
Harwich Port, 22, 43
Heel, 28, 50
Herreshof, 54; S-boats, 118
Hess, Jamie, 117, 127
Higham, Doug, 126–129
Highland Light, 115
High pressure systems, 12, 99, 103, 112
Hickley yawl, 78
Hurricane buoys, 83, 84
Hyannis, 15; ferry, 51
Hyannis Port, 43, 44, 54

Idem gaff-riggers, 118

Jib, 7; picnic jib, 49
Jibe, jibing, 5, 6, 12, 42, 51, 58

Keel, 49
Kennedy, John F., 118
Knot (nautical mile), 38
Knots, 13

Laser, 8, 19, 38, 71
Leinbach, Gus, 72
Lifejackets, 24, 41, 44
Lightning, 41
Line, 7
Little Island, 79

Long Island Sound, 73
Long Point, 135
Lovell, Tirzah, 129
Low pressure system, 12, 98, 99, 102
Luff up, 44

Main sheet, 12, 49, 50, 58
Marblehead, 22, 132, 139
Marstons Mill river, 83
Martha's Vineyard, 47, 50
Massachusetts Bay, 98, 111
Mast, 71; partners, 41; step, 33, 41;
    touching overhead power lines,
    41
Melcher, Jim, 56–57
Mellon's Cove, 79
Minot's Ledge, 111
Monetti, Bobby, 72
Monomoy Point, 22
Moon, and tide, 103–106
Mooring, 5–7, 13; inner and outer,
    113–114
Morris Island, 22, 128

Namskaket Creek, 113
Nantucket Sound, 10, 14, 36, 47, 78,
    80, 83, 102, 110, 111
Nauset Beach, 115
Newport, RI, 25
North Bay, 37, 77, 79, 83, 84
North Truro, 113

Oak Bluffs, 15, 47, 50, 51
Onset, 139
Orleans, 56, 115
OSTAR transatlantic race, 20
Osterville, 58, 82, 119, 127, 129
Outer Beach, 115–116
Outhaul, 87
Oyster Harbors, 50, 52, 79, 83

Patsy, 120
Plastic, boat covers, 62; boats, 62
Pleasant Bay, 22, 56, 128
Plymouth, 22, 111
Point Gammon, 23, 43, 45
Pollock Rip, 22
Poponesset, 83
Port, 7
Pram, 18

Prince's Cove, 83
Provincetown, 111–116; monument,
    135; wharf, 136

Quincy Bay, 114

Racing, 65–70; dangers in, 41
Radio direction finder, 24
Reaching, 10
Richardson, Wyman, 115
Robinson, Robby, 5
Rock Harbor, 114
Rope, 7
Round up, 39
Rowboat, 45
Rudder, 7
Run, run free, 9, 39
Ryan family, 125

Safety harness, 42, 43, 139
Sagamore Bridge, 139
Sails, 86–97; dropping, to anchor, 29
Sampson's Island, 80–82
Sandwich, 111, 116, 139
Scuppers, 50
Seapuit River, 37, 79, 80–81
Self-steer, 15, 51
Senior, Wianno, 14, 15, 17, 43, 48,
    51, 73, 77, 117–131
Sesuit Harbor, 114
Sheets, 7
Ship-to-shore radio, 24
Singlehanding, 43
Slocum, Joshua, 17
Small family, 123–125
Sole, 51
Solo, 18
South Atlantic, 106
South Bay, 77
Sou'wester, 39; smoky, 35
Spray, 17
Stage Harbor, 128
Starboard, 7
Star class, 118
Stern, 7
Stops, 7, 48
Succonnesset Shoal, 51–52
Sun, and tide, 103–106
Sunfish, 19, 114
Swinging room, 29, 30

Bog
Pond

Dam Pond

St. Mary's Island

Ishem Pond

Bay Street Boat Ramp

Crosby Yacht Inc.

Chester Crosby Boatyard

OSTERVILLE

EAST BAY

LITTLE
ISLAND

Oyster
Shanty

Wianno Yacht Club

Phinney's
Bay

Wright's Point

"SOUTH" BAY

WEST BAY

Aunt
Tempy's
Pond

Neck Pond

Crystal
Lake

Garrison's Point

Tower

Channel

Eel River

Seaview Avenue

Wianno Beach

The Cut